MINING STORIES

The Story of Industrial America Series
1850's - 1950's
Volume One

MINING STORIES

The Story of Industrial America Series

1850's - 1950's

Volume One

Jim Kissane

Published by

Fruition Press
5667 Kingfish Dr., Suite B,
Lutz, FL 33558
877-343-7907

Cover Image Credit: [New Railroad], 1916, Frank and Frances Carpenter collection (Library of Congress).

"The Story of Industrial America" is a selection of historically inspired works describing people, places and events of several specific major American industries of the 1850's through 1950's.

Each volume is lavishly illustrated with archival photos and drawings and includes glossary of industrial terms and an extensive reading list along with author commentary on the sources for the stories.

Readers will enjoy volumes containing original short stories about Automobiles, Communications, Construction, Electricity, Iron and Steel, Logging and Lumber, Manufacturing, Material Handling, Meatpacking, Mining, Motor Trucks, Oil and Gas, Railroads, Textiles, Transportation, Trolleys and Inter-urbans, and a special selection about America's "Western Expansion" during this era.

ISBN: 979-8-9874326-3-1

This book was produced with editorial guidance and technical support from Self-Publishing Consultant Robin Moore. To learn more about gaining assistance on the pathway to publishing before a world-wide readership on the Amazon platform, visit: www.robin-moore.com

Gold foil art on cover from Vecteezy.com

CONTENTS

INTRODUCTION

MY FAMILY'S roots go deep into the coal mines of Pennsylvania.

As I grew up, I listened to the stories of these unforgettable experiences, told by relatives and friends at family and community gatherings in my hometown. These tales entered my young ears and filled my imagination, evoking powerful images.

I can still close my eyes and see the dark, dusty tunnels which gave me a visceral sense of the miners' challenging and hazardous working conditions.

I can still recall the image of the miners, emerging from the depths of the earth at the end of their long and exhausting shifts, covered in dirt and sweat. I was awed by their resilience and their determination to work in such demanding circumstances.

I can't forget how the rugged landscape was dotted with mining towns where the company housing was built for the employers' convenience and as a way of controlling the lives of the hard-working families. I know now that, despite the hardships, this way of life created a close-knit community and a sense of accomplishment and genuine pride.

Those childhood stories served as a constant reminder that these were people with grit and determination who possessed immense physical and mental strength. The workers in the mines had to endure challenging conditions, including cramped spaces, poor ventilation and the constant risk of injury and death due to accidents. The dangerous nature of underground mining was ever-present and the families lived with constant fear and anxiety, knowing that their loved ones could die from cave-ins, explosions and toxic gases. At the end of each shift, the families gave thanks that their miners had come home alive and stoically accepted the consequences of this profession's grisly accidents or chronic health issues.

I came to admire the camaraderie and solidarity of these workers. Working in close-knit teams, they had to rely on each other for support and safety. It was a world of exhaustion and fatigue. Work in the mines was physically demanding and often required long hours of labor in harsh conditions.

This is an original collection of mining tales, describing a view of life at different kinds of mines across America, and a peek into the lives of people that were involved in these ventures. I challenge you to find another collection of mining stories that provides this kind of perspective.

I hope you will come to understand why I became so fascinated with the lives of those who made their living underground, toiling in perpetual darkness. It was a life of relentless physical exertion, exhaustion and danger. They endured hardships and made sacrifices that the human mind can scarcely comprehend.

Why did they do it?

It is important to remember that, during this era of our nation's history, the miner's life was one of hope and aspiration. The miners I describe pursued their work to provide a better life for themselves and their families. They labored to escape poverty and improve their living conditions. This hope enabled them to sustain their commitment to this complex and dangerous work.

My early exposure to the mining business taught me that these people had incredible fortitude and took enormous pride in their work. Beyond what they were paid, they shared a sense of accomplishment because they were extracting valuable resources from deep in the earth. They felt that they had earned the nation's respect because they were making an essential contribution to America's industrial progress.

While this is a work mostly about the miners, I would be remiss if I didn't acknowledge the incredible skill and talents of the foremen, mining engineers and others who had extensive training for underground mining operations. I will share the stories of these amazing individuals in an upcoming volume in this series.

But now, come with me to the mines and meet the people who undertook this dangerous and unpredictable work and risked their lives in the hopes that their underground world would lead to a better life.

A BIT OF AN ODDBALL

TO THE townsfolk of Newry, Maine, the appearance of this strangely-dressed fellow coming into town on this late summer afternoon in 1890 was a bit of a surprise. While a lone stranger coming into town wasn't that unusual, the attire of this odd fellow caused many raised eyebrows.

Newry, a quaint town of about eight hundred residents, was situated in a lush and beautiful valley in western Maine, surrounded by mountains. Much of the town's income came from agriculture as well as the local logging and lumber industry. But there were also several gemstone mining operations. A few were large mines, but most were smaller, each employing fewer than a dozen miners. Many wondered if this strange fellow was coming down from one of the local mines.

Everyone knew that most of the smaller mines around Newry were in remote and relatively inaccessible areas and that getting to and from these small mining operations involved traveling along rough trails and navigating through dense forests and rugged, rocky terrain. So most mining camps sent a man with a pack animal into town every few weeks to secure what the camp needed. While this fellow was dressed somewhat like a working miner, he had no pack animal and was carrying only a well-worn leather valise.

Anyone who was watching noticed that he strode down the main street with a definite sense of purpose. He seemed to be heading toward the General Store.

Each step he took was accompanied by a noticeable limp, reflected by a painful grimace on his face. His worn and sweat-stained attire also stood out from the work clothes worn by local farmers, shopkeepers, tradespeople, and lumbermen.

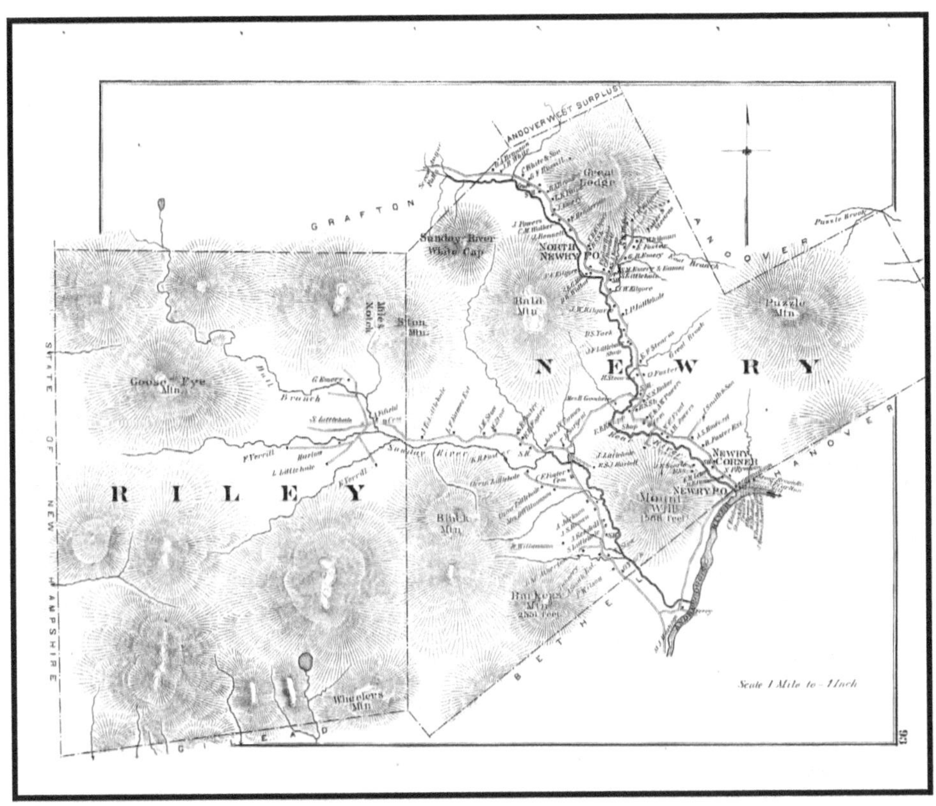

NEWRY MAINE

People took notice of his dirty, patched canvas work shirt and trousers, with poorly stitched leather patches on the knees. He wore a dusty bowler hat which partially covered his head of bright red hair. As he passed by the townsfolks on the wood plank sidewalks, they could pick up the odor of someone who had not bathed in quite some time.

While he didn't appear to be dangerous, he certainly was different.

None dared to step forward to greet him, let alone engage him in conversation. Parents drew their small children close and some hurriedly crossed with their families to the other side of the street. At the General Store, he silently shoved a pencil-scratched list of his needs to the proprietor and, as his order was filled, paid the proprietor in cash and carefully packed his supplies into his leather valise. Then, without conversation, he turned and began his return trip back up the mountain.

His rugged attire, while certainly not fashionable, was functional. He wasn't wearing average miner's apparel but looked very much like what a city person would wear with hasty adjustments to enable working in the mines. And that observation would be correct. His worn canvas work shirt had long sleeves, needed to protect his arms from the rough surfaces of the inside of the mine, and his coveralls, with the several poorly-stitched leather patches on the knees, provided needed protection while picking away on the rough, uneven tunnel floor.

The sturdy work boots he purchased that day at the General Store had thick soles to provide the traction a miner needed in the slippery tunnels and to protect his feet from falling rocks and other hazards in the mine.

As the townsfolk watched him begin his trip back up the mountain, they wondered, "Who is this strange fellow?"

Some miners working at the larger mines lived in town and traveled to and from work each day. But the miners who worked in the more distant mines further up the mountain stayed in miners' camps because trips to town could take several hours over challenging terrain, even in the best weather conditions.

In the miners' camps in all of the surrounding

mountains, you would find many "strange" persons because mining camps, in general, tended to attract a broad range of individuals, including people who were drawn to the prospect of striking it rich, those seeking adventure or escape from their previous lives, and others who may have been down on their luck and looking for work.

But for the most part, these men were hidden away from the townspeople of Newry.

The town gossip said she had heard from the proprietor of the General Store that all he knew about the new stranger was that he had recently started to work at a small mine up the side of the mountain that had been abandoned a while back. It had been recently claimed and was being re-opened by the owner of a neighboring mine.

This was not an unusual situation. Several small mines in the area operated intermittently, with some producing for only a short period before being abandoned. In general, the mines around Newry were small-scale operations that were often under-capitalized and subject to fluctuating prices for the minerals and metals they produced. Operators of gemstone mines in Maine in the 1880's had their fair share of challenges from a lack of infrastructure, difficult terrain, and limited access to transportation. These factors made it challenging for many mines to operate profitably and sustainably. Miners tended to come and go.

While most workers in Newry were involved with agriculture, logging, and lumber, gemstone mining was a smaller but important part of the local economy.

In the late 1880's, Victorian buyers had created a growing demand for colorful gemstones, including minerals like quartz, feldspar, mica, beryl, tourmaline, and spodumene. Among the more sought-after ores being mined was tourmaline, a gemstone highly valued at that time for its beauty. It was also said that these crystals had magical healing powers.

But from a miner's viewpoint, finding valuable tourmaline was not easy. When first extracted from the underground tunnels, tourmaline ore appeared rough and unremarkable, with a dull or opaque surface and little or no color. The mountains around Newry had promising veins of tourmaline. And from certain mines, ore was being recovered that was considered to be very valuable.

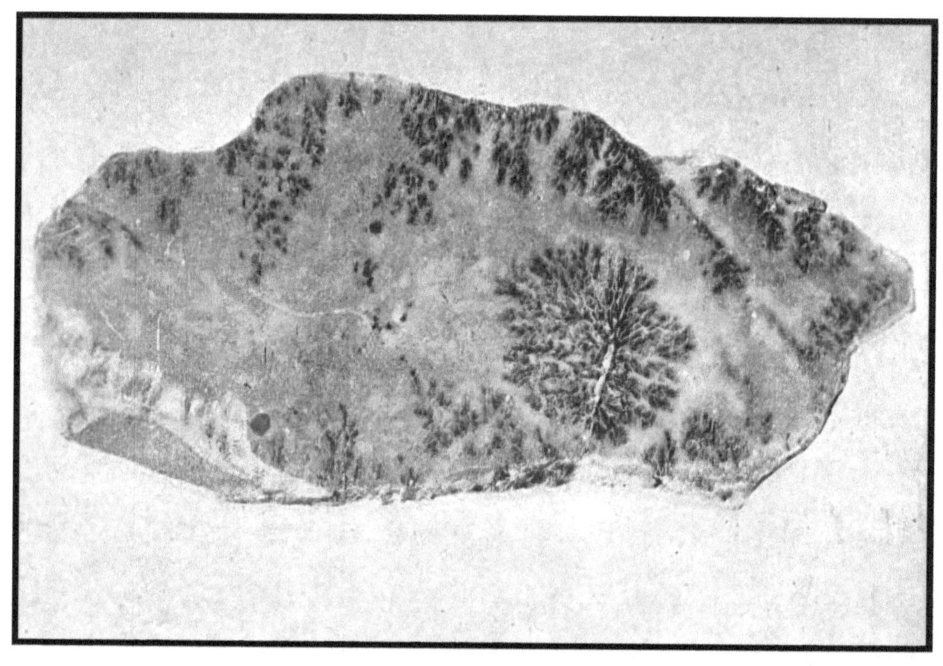

TOURMALINE ORE

But it wasn't easy to find and extract this high-quality ore. Even experienced miners admitted that finding the right geological conditions for tourmaline formation was difficult.

The mine owner had mentioned at the Assay Offices in Bethel and Newry that a recently-hired man named Samuel had a sharp eye and could spot tourmaline's elongated crystal shape concealed in the presence of other minerals and materials, such as quartz, feldspar, and mica. And, unlike the other miners in the area, Samuel had shown that he had the skill to extract the tourmaline crystals from the surrounding rock without breaking them, using only the most basic mining equipment such as pickaxes, hand drills, and hammers.

The new mine owner had good reason to be pleased.

He had not had to pay much for the abandoned mine. Its remote location and small size made this property much less attractive to buyers. Mines that were located in more accessible areas commanded a higher purchase price.

Every day, at this small mine, Samuel and the

nine other miners would enter the mine and go to a particular section which they felt had potential and work that section until quitting time. Hour after hour, they would pick away at the rock, extracting chunks of ore and load them onto a nearby mine car. When the car was full, they would push or pull the car along the wooden rails on the floor of the tunnel to a designated location just outside the mouth of the mine.

As the new mine owner looked over the daily production reports, he was pleased with the performance of this new miner named Samuel. According to mine records which had been left by the previous owner, even though Samuel was working in an older and distant section of the mine, he was somehow finding productive veins of quality tourmaline ore.

"Strange," the owner thought, "The old mine records indicate that this part of the mine had been previously worked a couple of years ago, yet this Samuel fellow has returned and found significant quantities of quality ore in that area."

A couple of months after the new owner re-opened the mine, seeing evidence of significant potential in his recent acquisition, he hired a new mine foreman named Clancy to oversee its operations.

When Clancy appeared at the mine, he started assessing the operation for which he was now responsible.

At the end of each day's shift, all the miners would come out of the mine to the small office where their daily production was reviewed and each miner would receive their day's wages. A miner was paid based on the number of loaded ore cars they brought up after each shift. At this mine, the cars were as small as the tunnels were narrow, measuring only about two feet wide and four feet long. These cars, when filled, were pushed or pulled by the miner to the surface. Each carried about 300 pounds of extracted ore.

As each car was brought to the surface, the foreman inspected the quality and quantity of the tourmaline ore as it was unloaded from the mine car and checked for any signs of waste or impurities. Then he made a record in an entry into that day's production log, including the miner's name and what part of the mine this ore had come from.

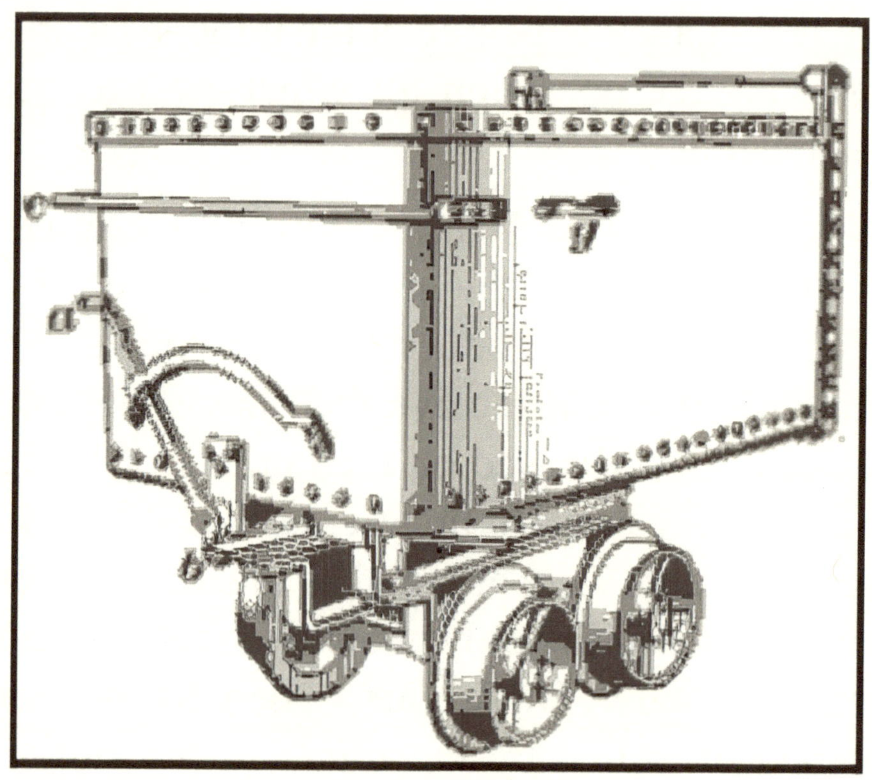

ORE CAR

Day after day, Samuel's cars were full of tourmaline ore showed signs of good quality tourmaline; a rich, vibrant color and seemingly free of cracks or other imperfections. Clancy noted that Samuel consistently was the last man out of the mine at the end of each shift.

After collecting his wages and receipt, Samuel would quietly and swiftly retreat up the hillside to his small shanty.

Beyond the recording the weight and apparent quality of ore coming from each section of the mine each shift, Clancy had found it helpful to know a bit about his miners. He had an experienced eye for assessing miners and since he had not hired these men, he wanted to get to know them a little better.

With an experienced and observant eye, Clancy would watch each miner as they exited the mine each day.

Upon leaving the darkness of the mine, they would take a few moments for their eyes to adjust to the daylight, catch their breath, store their mining tools in the tool shed, and go to the nearby pitcher pump to wash up. They then headed over to the mine office to get paid for the day's work, after which, two or three at a time, they would head over to the miner's camp. Samuel, always the last to leave the mine, avoided discussion with other miners waiting to get paid. Once paid, he would head in a different direction, up a steep hillside trail, in a different direction from the miner's camp.

Clancy was curious and sensed he needed to learn more about this strange miner.

Clancy had a custom of dropping over to the miners' camps. He enjoyed watching them share their meals and leisure activities. This was the part of his job that he most enjoyed.

In the evening, when he visited in the miner's camp, he would observe miners reading and passing around newspapers, books, and other printed materials. Often a few miners were engaged in card games, and usually, one miner in each camp entertained others by playing a fiddle, banjo, or harmonica and inviting others to sing along. Clancy welcomed the chance to sit around a fire with his miners as they shared stories about their lives and experiences.

MINER'S CAMP

These informal interactions taught him that the other miners knew little about this Samuel fellow. They had invited Samuel to join them at their camp but he refused these invitations. Some wondered if this fellow had some dark secret. Maybe he was a fugitive or was a bit crazy. Others felt he might just be a quiet loner.

Clancy was now convinced that he needed to know more about this Samuel character.

So the following day, Clancy followed Samuel into the mine to see what he was up to. Clancy was shocked to find Samuel digging in a spot where according to mine records, there was said to be no known viable ore vein. Keeping in the shadows of the tunnel, he watched Samuel feverishly dig deeper and deeper, seemingly oblivious to everything around him.

At the end of the shift, as Clancy looked over the ore cars which had been brought topside, he was astounded to find that Samuel's cars had some of the best-looking ore he had ever seen. How was Samuel able to get this quantity of high-quality ore that was supposed to be "played out"?

He continued to watch Samuel in that section for the next couple of days and to Clancy's surprise, each day's production was even richer than the day before.

On the third day, Clancy came up behind Samuel and asked what he was doing. Samuel looked up at him with a sad expression and said, "If you must know, I'm digging to find the body of my fiancée."

The foreman was taken aback.

"Your fiancée? What do you mean?" he asked.

Samuel explained that he was certain his fiancée, who was named Alice, had been lost in that mine two years ago.

He said that her father, who had owned and operated the mine for almost thirty years, had died of natural causes and his daughter, his sole heir, was supposed to take over the mine. She lived in Boston, where she and Samuel had first met several years earlier.

One week before receiving word of her father's passing, Samuel had asked Alice to marry him. She accepted and the couple was anxious to tell the family about their plans. But, since Thanksgiving was only three weeks away, they decided that the upcoming holiday and family gathering would be an excellent time to share the good news.

When Alice received the notice by telegram of her father's passing, she immediately bought a train ticket to Newry. It wasn't a long journey, only about six hours, taking the Boston and Maine Railroad which served both cities. Samuel, who had a job as a laborer at a Boston factory, would not accompany her. His employer expected workers to work long hours, sometimes up to twelve hours a day, six days a week. Taking time off from work for personal reasons, such as illness or family obligations, was discouraged and workers were punished for taking time off. Even a request could result in loss of seniority or even termination. As the couple was looking at starting a new life together, they discussed the situation and agreed Samuel should stay behind and she would be back within a week after settling her father's affairs.

When Alice arrived in Newry, she decided that the first thing she would do was to hike up to the mine. She hadn't been in it since childhood and felt being in the mine would help her connect with her father. She wandered deep into the mine with only a lantern, looking at its condition. When she was deep into one of the headings, the tunnel collapsed behind her, and she found herself sealed inside the mine.

Other than Samuel, no one knew she was in town. Thus, they could not have known about her excursion to the closed mine. So no one would be coming to help her.

As court records reflected, the mine owner had passed away, and the only family member was notified but failed to respond. After sixty days, the mine was designated as "abandoned."

The mine sat idle as many abandoned mines did for quite some time. Meanwhile, Samuel, still in

Boston, had enquired about Alice in Newry, but no one could tell him whether she had ever arrived, let alone her whereabouts.

Mr. Berry, who owned several small mines in western Maine, knew of the quality tourmaline Alice's father had been retrieving from his mine. When the court declared this mine "abandoned," he submitted a purchase offer to the court.

In the more than three months since Alice's unexplained disappearance, Samuel spent each Sunday, which was his only day off, trying to re-trace Alice's journey to Newry. He wasn't getting any answers. When he arrived in Newry, none of the townspeople had any recollection of seeing Alice. Week after week, Sunday after Sunday, Samuel tirelessly looked for answers to what might have happened to his fiancée. On his third trip back to Newry, he produced the telegram Alice had received from the court clerk containing her father's death notice. Samuel asked everyone, hoping to uncover some scrap of information about where Alice might have gone during her visit. A lady who overheard

Samuel inquiring about Alice recognized the father's name and told Samuel about the mine.

It seemed like a strange place to search but Samuel was desperate for any clue which might lead him to solve the mystery of her disappearance.

Samuel had never been in any mine, but with the directions the locals provided, he immediately wanted to head up the side of the mountain. The lady he had just met warned him against making such an unprepared trip. She told him it could take him the better part of the afternoon to get to the mine and suggested that he take along some basic provisions. Given the time of day, the General Store was not open, so the kind lady provided him with an old leather valise containing some bread, a rope, and a lantern.

Samuel thanked her and set off in great haste. The primitive trail to where the mine was said to be was steep and rocky, with numerous switchbacks and challenging terrain. Samuel, fit but inexperienced, climbed higher up the mountain and the terrain became increasingly rugged and exposed. He had to circumvent the many steep cliffs and rocky outcroppings carefully and by the time he arrived at the location of the mine, he had slipped several times but had been able to avoid falls and other life-threatening hazards.

Nightfall was upon him and he spent the evening just inside the opening to the mine. The next morning, the new owner awakened him, asking him about his business.

"So, are you applying for the miner's job I posted in Newry?" the owner asked.

Samuel had not seen this posted notice but, without hesitation, nodded and said, "Yes, Sir, I am."

The man looked him up and down. "You sure don't look like a miner."

Samuel said, "Why don't you put me to work and I'll show you what I can do."

And with that, Samuel was put to work in the mine.

When Samuel finished his story, Clancy was moved to tears by his this man's quest to finding his lost love. Clancy had himself suffered a loss; his wife had passed due to consumption two years before. He understood Samuel's pain.

DIGGING TOGETHER

Immediately, Clancy returned to the tool shed at the mine opening, collected a rock drill and pick and helped Samuel dig in that heading together. The two dug for several more days, but they never found anything. Eventually, Clancy had to return to his duties but he promised Samuel that he would keep the search going and said he felt sure that they would find her remains someday.

In his still-frequent evening visits to his miner's campsites, Clancy told the others Samuel's story. From that day on, the other miners looked at the man they regarded as so strange with new eyes. They realized that he wasn't odd or pitiful, just a tormented man consumed by grief and searching for closure.

They began to include him in their conversations and invite him to their gatherings. Samuel slowly but surely began to come out of his shell. Eventually, Samuel left his shanty and joined the other miners in their encampment.

Although they never found his fiancée, the search gave Samuel's life a purpose and helped him connect with the other miners in a way he never had before. Although he would always be seen as a bit of an oddball, the people of the mining community and the townsfolk in Newry grew to appreciate him for who he was, quirks and all. And the Tourmaline, a gem known and used for centuries for its alleged healing abilities, was now helping heal the huge hole in Samuel's heart.

A FLIP OF A COIN

SOMETIMES A person is faced with a life-changing decision. Young Amos Scott, a self-educated machinist from Rhode Island, was about to discover how challenging such a decision could be.

It was 1881 in Virginia City, Nevada and officials of the Savage Mining Company were becoming worried. After over two decades of productive silver mining of the Comstock Lode, silver market prices fell but production costs continued rising.

Increased competition was being felt by the other large silver mining operations working the Comstock Lode, and the "Big Four" investors were being more careful where they invested their money.

The Superintendent of the Savage Mine operation, John William Mackay, was a gregarious Irish-American who had introduced many innovations to the Savage Mine gleaned from his work overseas. Looking at the situation, he knew several changes in the operation of the Savage Mine needed to be made. One of these was reducing the considerable time and cost of bringing extracted silver ore to the surface.

TYPICAL COMSTOCK LODE MINE

The culprit was the depletion of high-grade ore deposits, the area's primary source of silver and gold. As the high-grade ore became scarcer, extracting precious metals became more expensive and challenging, leading to a decline in profitability for many mining companies. The Savage Mining company owners felt that Mackay was the right man for the job, enabling the mine to continue operations profitably.

The steam engines used to power the pumps, crushers and hoists of the Savage mine were older "Cornish style" steam engines, which Mackay realized were impacting the productivity of mine operations. This older type of engine had high fuel consumption, which made them expensive to operate and maintain due to their large size and the fact that they operated at high pressures. The records showed frequent breakdowns and delays in mining production due to these engines, which, even with regular maintenance, had breakdowns that caused a significant financial impact on the mine.

Mackay was looking for an innovation for his mine and saw a Corliss engine at the 1876 Centennial Exhibition in Philadelphia, Pennsylvania. He had become impressed at the power and efficiency of the Corliss design.

"My God!" he gasped at first sight of this behemoth.

CORLISS ENGINE AT 1876 CENTENNIAL IN PHILADELPHIA

The double engine that Corliss had built and erected in the Machinery Hall of the Exposition was enormous: over forty feet high and weighing some six hundred tons. It produced fifteen-hundred horsepower, a number unheard of in that day.

Each cylinder of this massive engine had a diameter of forty inches and a stroke of ten feet, and each drove a walking beam that was twenty-five feet long and weighed eleven tons. The fifty-six-ton flywheel which made thirty-six revolutions per minute was just under thirty feet in diameter and drove a nearly ten-foot pinion gear that weighed eight and a half tons.

The gigantic Corliss engine was said to drive some five miles of overhead line shafting throughout the Exhibition Hall and provided power to an estimated eight thousand machines.

Skeptics claimed that it was impossible to build such an engine. And the Exposition Committee had a great deal at risk. On the Exposition's opening day, with Mackay in attendance, many notables were on hand, including U.S. President Ulysses S. Grant and his guest, Emperor Dom Pedro II of Brazil.

As the moment for starting the engine approached, the large crowd fell silent. President Grant and Emperor Dom Pedro II each threw a lever. Steam hissed into the cylinders, the floor shook, the massive flywheel turned slowly and the walking beams of the engine moved.

Connected to the Corliss engine was a "line shaft" that ran the length of the massive exhibit hall. The line shaft was a long, rotating metal shaft attached below the exhibit hall floor and was powered by the stationary Corliss steam engine. When turning, it transmitted power to various machines and tools in the hall through a system of belts and pulleys attached to it by belts. In the 19th century, overhead line shafts were in common use and allowed a single power source to drive multiple machines simultaneously, increasing manufacturing operations' efficiency and productivity.

When the main drive belt to the line shaft was engaged at the Corliss engine, the line shaft machinery attached throughout the hall got busy sewing clothes, printing newspapers, sawing lumber, and doing a thousand other jobs. Amidst all this "busy-ness," the lone attendant sitting atop the Corliss engine sat in a chair on the platform, reading a newspaper!

MACHINES RUNNING ON OVERHEAD LINE SHAFT

When the main drive belt to the line shaft was engaged at the Corliss engine, the line shaft machinery attached throughout the hall got busy sewing clothes, printing newspapers, sawing lumber, and doing a thousand other jobs. Amidst all this "busy-ness," the lone attendant sitting atop the Corliss engine sat in a chair on the platform, reading a newspaper!

Seeing this spectacle, there was not a single moment of hesitation in Mackay's mind.

"I must have this engine for the Savage Mine," he thought.

He dashed off a telegraph message to the founders and Board of Directors of the Savage Mining Company to that effect.

After a conversation with Corliss at the Exhibition, he learned of the additional benefits of the Corliss engine over the steam engines currently being used at the Savage mine.

Not only did this engine surpass the output of the Cornish engine being used but the efficiency and economies of this new engine were irresistible.

Yes, it would be a significant investment, estimated in 1881 to be in the low six figures (equating to several million dollars in today's values). Still, Mackay felt it was essential to remain competitive in a tightening market.

By the time he returned to Virginia City, Mackay had crafted a detailed proposal for a custom Corliss engine to be built for the Savage Mine. The management and board agreed and placed an order for the new engine.

George H. Corliss, the inventor and founder of the Corliss steam engine, understood the importance of this transaction. He dispatched one of his apprentices, a young fellow named Amos, to visit the mine location and assess the operational and installation requirements.

Corliss was born to a farming family in Easton, Massachusetts, on June 2, 1817.

He began an apprenticeship with a local millwright named Otis Tufts at sixteen. Here, he gained practical experience working with machines and tools. He later moved to Troy, New York, where he worked as a machinist and continued developing his engineering and invention skills. According to historical records, Corliss began working with Tufts as an apprentice in a machine shop in Easton, Massachusetts, in

1837. During this time, Corliss developed his mechanical skills and experimented with steam engines, which would later lead to his development of the Corliss steam engine. He had little formal education but had a natural talent for mechanics and engineering, evident from an early age.

In 1848, he established the Corliss Steam Engine Company in Providence, Rhode Island, which became his engineering and invention work base.

The Corliss steam engine, considered among his best-known inventions, was a global phenomenon for having significant improvements over earlier steam engines available in the day.

One of the most unusual things about Corliss was his obsessive attention to detail and insistence on precision in his work.

Corliss was a perfectionist, evident in the years he spent designing and perfecting his steam engine, which he patented in 1849. The Corliss steam engine was notable for its efficiency and reliability, and it quickly became highly popular in industrial applications.

Corliss had several apprentices working under him who were being trained in various engineering aspects, including the design and construction of steam engines, machine tools, and other industrial equipment. Corliss believed strongly in the importance of apprenticeship to pass on knowledge and skills to the next generation of engineers and machinists.

Besides his work as an inventor and engineer, Corliss also advocated for vocational education and training. He believed that a well-trained workforce was essential for the continued growth and prosperity of the American economy. As a result, he played an active role in promoting apprenticeship programs and vocational schools throughout the United States.

Amos had apprenticed under Mr. Corliss's direct supervision for several years. During that time, he acquired an extensive range of technical skills, including significant knowledge of different types and styles of steam engines. In his years of working under his mentor, Amos obtained a thorough understanding of the principles and operation of various steam engines. He was very familiar with the basic mechanics of steam engine design, the function of the multiple components, and the principles of heat transfer.

Beyond this basic knowledge, under Mister Corliss' tutelage, Amos now also possessed a detailed understanding of not only what it took to build such an engine but also what it took to maintain and repair the engine, including the routine tasks of cleaning, lubrication, and replacement of damaged or worn-out parts.

Additionally, since his years of apprenticeship included working in the company's foundry and machine shop, he had gained significant knowledge of metallurgy, machining, and welding practices.

Throughout this time, his mentor ensured that important safety considerations and practices could not be violated in every stage of design, manufacture, and operation.

So Amos became obsessive in observing and instructing others in all aspects of steam engine operations, including monitoring steam pressure, water levels, and temperature. These were all essential practices he knew were paramount in preventing accidents and ensuring the safe operation of a powerful steam engine.

Working side-by-side with Corliss, he was taught various troubleshooting techniques with the engine. He became adept at diagnosing and fixing any problems that might arise during operation, such as leaks or malfunctions in the engine or boiler.

Part of what gained Amos so much respect from his mentor was his incredible attention to the smallest detail. Seeing this unique quality, Corliss often invited Amos to help update the company's machine designs, detailed procedures, and logs for record keeping.

Corliss was very proud of Amos's growth

of knowledge and wisdom over the past several years and thought of him fondly as a protégé.

Corliss called his protégé aside after his return from the Exposition in Philadelphia.

"Amos, I expect to receive an order for a new engine from the Savage Mining Company in Nevada. As my most seasoned apprentice knowledgeable in my engine's operation and capabilities, I would like you to go out to Nevada and determine the requirements for this new engine, which they want."

Amos' face reddened at the compliment. "Thank you, Mister Corliss. I shall do my best. Is there anything special about this company or application?"

Corliss replied, "Yes, the Savage Mining Company is a huge and important silver mining operation. The company has a reputation for being demanding, so your technical skills and attention to detail may not be enough. I must warn you that your impressive gift of communication and diplomacy will be necessary. These can be some difficult people to deal with."

He pointed out that unlike the other new customers Amos had previously worked with in Eastern industries and mines, going into Savage's established operation would require a "special touch."

"I've met with their Superintendent of Mines, a Scottish fellow named Mackay. He won't stand for any nonsense.

JOHN WILLIAM MACKAY

"You'll not only have to prove to him and the mine owners that you are an expert operating engineer but able to interact effectively with other members of the Savage operating team. Mackay says they operate differently out west and like doing things their way. So right off the bat, you can expect to be challenged by the mine's firemen, boiler operators, and other mining engineers. They've gotten used to how things work, and this engine will be a big change.

"But remember, you are there to coordinate the safe and efficient introduction and operation of the Corliss engine in a large production mine setting. Your job is to make them comfortable with a new way of doing things. Think you can do that?"

"Mister Corliss, I know I can," and with a giant smile, he turned and left for the main office to secure his travel arrangements and funding for the trip.

Amos had a great deal of self-confidence. Since childhood, he had a solid understanding of mathematics and science. Under Corliss, he gained additional insights into machine design, including tutoring in physics and thermodynamics, all necessary to understand the principles behind the Corliss engine's operation.

These were also essential to make appropriate calculations for the engine's operation, maintenance, and repair.

But unlike most of the other apprentices, Amos had come from a Boston family of some social standing, and from this environment, he could engage with influential and powerful people from all walks of life. His father had taught him the delicate skills of diplomacy and negotiation, and Amos was a quick learner.

When Corliss hand-picked Amos to go to Virginia City, his young protégé eagerly jumped at the chance, as demonstrated by his eagerness to show his mentor what he could do.

The following day Amos appeared at the train station carrying two bags, his traveling bag with his personal effects and a large leather valise containing sensitive measurement and recording equipment, some basic hand tools, and several notebooks. Amos embarked on the journey to Virginia City.

Traveling from Providence, Rhode Island to Virginia City, Nevada, was a long and challenging journey. The distance between the two cities across the country was approximately twenty-seven hundred miles and involved a trip of several weeks. The first leg was by train from Providence, Rhode Island to New York, New York, then onto Chicago, and then to San Francisco. The last leg involved a stagecoach that connected with the Virginia & Truckee Railroad Depot, completing the trip to Virginia City, Nevada.

Upon reaching Virginia City with his valises and letter of introduction from George Corliss, he presented himself at the company offices, where he met Mackay. Both men were taken aback. Mackay was known throughout the mining industry for his imposing physical stature and distinctive appearance. A tall man, he stood around six feet four inches with a robust build and broad shoulders. Amos' upward gaze into

Mackay's piercing blue eyes and a thick, bushy, three-pronged beard projected a style of face he had never seen back East. Beyond his facial appearance, he wore formal clothing, which seemed very out of place in a mining community.

Mackay stared back at this smallish figure, awkwardly introducing himself by extending his hand. At five and a half feet tall, Amos was about the same height as the European and Chinese workers who worked in his mine, but those men were muscular and rugged. This bookish fellow seemed to be anything but.

In this mind, he wondered, "Whom has Corliss sent me?"

In a deep and resonant voice, he introduced himself, "The name's Mackay and I'm the Superintendent of Mines here at the Savage Mining Company. Come with me."

He ushered Amos into Mackay's sizable but not pretentious office, offering him a comfortable leather chair.

"So, Mister Scott, I understand that Mister Corliss has sent you to us to evaluate the requirements for our new steam engine."

Offering forth his letter of introduction with a steady hand, Amos nodded and began.

"Yes, I have worked under Mister Corliss' direction for the past fifteen years, and I have the greatest knowledge of his engine and its applications in the company."

Mackay studied the letter of introduction, set it face down on his desk, and gazed at a map of the Savage mine that hung on the nearby wall. "What do you know of mining operations, Mister Scott?"

"Over the past three years, we have installed several of our engines in coal mines back east … various applications, mainly pumping, crushing, and hoisting."

Mackay nodded his head, and his face relaxed a bit. "What do you know about our situation here, Mister Scott?"

Amos smiled and said, "Most of my colleagues just call me Amos. Since I expect you and I will work closely over the next several months, please feel free to call me Amos if you like.

"But to answer your question, I have read what has been published about the Comstock Lode, and my understanding is that Savage is one of the larger and most productive operations working the Comstock, along with Consolidated Virginia, California, Chollar, and Crown Point Mines."

"What's your impression of the Comstock Lode, Amos?"

"The Savage, at thirty-eight hundred feet deep, seems to be one of the deepest mines, and I sense that with it, there are some challeng-es that other mines do not have. Hoisting and pumping operations, for example. But I've no-ticed Savage has always been a leader in mining innovation. Unless I'm wrong, wasn't Savage a pioneer in using pneumatic drills and develop-ing the square-set timbering method to shore up the mine's tunnels?"

By now, Mackay's face had relaxed, and a faint smile appeared on his lips.

"Excellent, Amos," he said, "I see you have done your homework on us."

"Yes sir, my mentor trained me well to consider every relevant detail."

"You seem pretty sure of yourself."

Amos reached into his pocket and flipped a shiny silver dollar into the air.

"I am. Are you willing to wager that I will get it right?"

Mackay replied, "Mister Scott, I'm not a gambling man, but I have been known to take a calculated risk. I sense you know what you are doing."

Mackay arose and invited Amos to join him. As the two exited his office, he motioned to his assistant, saying, "Would you please take Mister Scott to our hotel and ensure he gets properly settled in?"

And with a firm handshake, he closed by saying, "Amos, I think I am going to enjoy working with you. Can we continue our conversation over breakfast tomorrow morning? I'm sure the journey here has you looking for a good night's sleep."

Amos smiled and nodded as he turned and said, "Yes, a good night's sleep is just what the doctor ordered."

The following day began at five o'clock. He arose, made his morning preparations and was at a table in the hotel dining room when Mackay arrived. His arrival was extraordinary. Not only did his imposing figure stride into the room in formal attire, but he was adorned by a silk top hat. It was not what Amos had expected at all. It turned out it was the signature attire for Mackay and considered a hallmark of his persona.

As the two met and discussed the plan for gathering the necessary requirements, Amos captured all the names and particulars of where he should go and whom he would meet. At seven O'clock sharp, Mackay checked his ornately carved silver pocket watch, concluded the breakfast and strode briskly to his next appointment.

For the next several weeks, Amos worked in all sections of the mine, taking measurements, recording data and taking notes about the needs of the mining operation. Every week, he would have breakfast with Mackay in the hotel dining room, discussing his findings and observations. At the end of the fourth week, he completed his technical analysis and had a final wrap-up meeting with Mackay in his office, laying out what he felt were the next steps.

Amos was a very clear communicator. He described to Mackay what he had considered and, on each point, obtained agreement that his review of the operation had been thorough and accurate. Mackay stood up and directed Amos to the company telegrapher, who arranged for some of the most critical study data to be sent back to company headquarters in Providence, Rhode Island.

The following morning, Mackay and Amos

said their goodbyes as Amos boarded his train at the Virginia & Truckee Railroad Depot.

The arduous journey of the next four weeks back to Rhode Island provided Amos some quiet time to collect his thoughts about his experience and impressions while in Virginia City. It had exposed him to a world, unlike anything he had previously encountered. During his time at the mine, he had not only met with people able to assist him with the technical information he needed to prepare engine specifications but was introduced by Mackay to several other significant players who were active in working the Comstock Lode.

He was also introduced to the founders of the Savage Mining Company, William Sharon, William Ralston, and James B. Flood, also known as the "Bonanza Kings," who had experienced tremendous success in mining the Comstock Lode. He found these men thought and acted quite differently than the captains of industry he had been exposed to back east.

He had developed an admiration for the pioneering entrepreneurial spirit of these self-made men who were willing to take risks and innovate no matter the circumstances to succeed.

Unlike his eastern counterparts, these men seemed to do bold things without the restrictions imposed by distant Boards of Directors, bankers, and attorneys. When these men saw an opportunity, their drive to create something new took center stage. They were less concerned with social acceptance or preserving reverence for traditional ways of doing business.

The spirit he felt was that of rugged individualism, a risk-taking mentality, and exciting entrepreneurial energy. He enjoyed working with these new people very much.

Upon his return to Providence, he became immersed in the new engine design for the Savage mine. Telegraphed from Virginia City to Providence before his departure, the work on the engine design had already begun. Working together with the company founder, the two worked long hours for almost three weeks to prepare design specifications.

The technical and service requirements of the Savage mine called for an adaptation of the Corliss engine design. When the design work was complete, Corliss submitted a quotation for a large stationary steam engine that weighed approximately one hundred twenty-five tons.

Because of its size, Corliss arranged for the initial engine to be manufactured by the William A. Harris Steam Engine Company in 1882 to power the Savage mine's hoisting machinery. The Savage mine engine had a cylinder bore of thirty-two inches and a stroke of eighty-four inches, capable of producing up to nine hundred horsepower.

They sent the specifications for the engine, the price proposal for the engine, and its installation at the mine to Mackay. It was in line with the earlier estimates and a contract to begin production was signed.

The Harris Steam Engine Company had a solid reputation for producing high-quality and innovative steam engines widely used in various industries, including marine, rail, and power generation. Although technically the two were competitors, the two firms had collaborated on several large projects. One of these, where Corliss and Harris partnered, was the construction of the steam engines for the Centennial Exhibition held in Philadelphia in 1876, where Mackay had first seen the Corliss engine. On this project, Corliss had designed the engines, while Harris handled their construction. The same relationship was used to construct the engines for the Savage mine.

Upon the engine's completion and test, it was disassembled for shipment to Virginia City. All of this was done under the watchful eye of George Corliss and Amos, now his deputy.

Amos accompanied the engine as it was loaded on the train for the journey westward. Because of the massive nature of the engine, special shipping arrangements had to be put in place, which were overseen personally by Amos.

Upon reaching San Francisco, Amos went to Virginia City to ensure the advance preparations he wired to Mackay were in order. Since his previous visit, Mackay and Amos regularly exchanged information every two weeks. Mackay kept him apprised of the detailed preparations underway in anticipation of the Corliss.

The Savage Shaft engine house into which the engine was to be assembled and put into service was an impressive structure, standing at one hundred ten feet tall and measuring seventy-five feet by one hundred ten feet in its base. The engine house was constructed of brick and stone and had a slate roof. The hoisting works were fifty-five feet tall and housed a massive double-drum hoist with twelve-foot-diameter steel wheels, which enabled the rapid hoisting of five thousand pounds of ore per trip.

The engine that powered the hoist was a forty-foot-high steam engine with a twelve-foot flywheel.

Amos understood the immense pressure that he would encounter upon his arrival.

But since he possessed detailed knowledge of the engine, by following this project from user requirements to design through manufacture, he was confident that upon delivery, he could progress with assembly, testing, and putting the Corliss into production in the shortest amount of time. Every day of downtime after the older Scottish engine was taken offline was costly to the company, and here's where his communications and diplomatic skills would be tested.

There was one area that Amos needed more hands-on experience, and that was supervision and management. For this project to proceed, he needed not only to plan each step of the installation and cutover process but also had to be on top of every person on the team that Mackay had provided for him.

Amos had confided in Mackay his concern about this area in his initial requirements survey trip.

"Mister Mackay, I do not have the experience of directing a team of men on such an important project as this. Is that going to be a problem?"

"No, Amos, I appreciate you being forthcoming with me. I will appoint a project superintendent to ensure you get any resources or cooperation needed in this effort. That man will report directly to me. Does that help?"

Amos, face reddened as he said, "Thank you, sir. I appreciate the confidence you have placed in me."

Mackay had high hopes and great expectations for this project since the time of the contract signing. He was prepared to secure the best people he knew would be necessary to complete this undertaking under Amos' guidance.

The Corliss engine that Savage had chosen was well-suited for the Savage Mine because of its high power output and efficiency. It was also a design that would be relatively easy to operate and maintain. But beneath its simplicity was a complex machine that would initially take precise effort to assemble and calibrate.

Mackay continued to collaborate by telegraph with Amos to ensure he had the right team onsite when the engine parts arrived. Mackay was a strong proponent of new communications technologies and had several investments in them.

Amos had instructed Mackay that upon his arrival with the engine components, he would require a team with the following capabilities.

He needed three reliable men with proven mechanical skills to help assemble the engine. These men were to have a thorough understanding of mechanical systems and the ability to work with metal parts, use hand tools, read technical drawings, and work with precision. A man with engineering knowledge, who understands valve timing, steam pressure, and the workings of various steam engine components, such as cylinders, pistons, and crankshafts, was essential.

The men selected needed physical strength, as assembling a steam engine requires much physical strength and endurance to handle heavy parts and machinery. Likewise, these men needed to have proven strong attention to detail. Assembling a sophisticated steam engine requires meticulous attention to detail, and each team member needs to ensure that all parts were assembled correctly and the engine operates smoothly.

Working underground and working topside call for a similar emphasis on safety. Steam engines of any design can be dangerous, so the team should know safety procedures when working around pressurized vessels.

As he had expected, one by one, Mackay assembled the team that Amos had requested, and once the components had all arrived, assembly began.

Piece by piece, the new engine took shape in the Shaft House. The team Mackay had assembled was very much to the liking of Amos, and they worked as smoothly together as well as the delicate design mechanism they were constructing.

Upon completing this task, Amos provided a journal for the Chief Operating Engineer's use that provided a way to record every aspect of the engine's operation and routine care and maintenance, including fuel consumption, maintenance schedules, and any issues that might arise during operation.

Mackay became increasingly impressed with Amos's intelligence and intuition with each phase of the project.

One day as the two were preparing to wrap up the day's work and head back to the hotel, he put his hand on Amos' shoulder. "Amos, I could always use a bright young fellow like you on my team!"

The relationship between Amos and Mackay evolved to a very different level throughout this undertaking. The brusque and demanding superintendent he had encountered at their first meeting had, like Corliss, taken him under his wing, taught him, encouraged him, and supported him. Amos felt the two, while certainly not equals, had a great deal of mutual respect and admiration for each other, and truth be told, Amos felt Mackay had been a friend and mentor to him.

Mackay's casual comment now put a vital career decision to the forefront of Amos' thinking. Amos spent many sleepless nights wrestling with his decision. He knew that either choice would have far-reaching consequences. He didn't want to make a mistake.

Ultimately, he decided to talk to Mister Corliss and ask for his advice.

"Mister Corliss, I've been agonizing over a difficult decision," he admitted, "I have had the good fortune to have received an offer of employment from Mister McKay. I feel quite conflicted in this situation because while you have spent so much time and effort educating and coaching me, this feels like an opportunity."

Corliss listened patiently as James explained the situation. He didn't try to sway Amos one way or the other but instead offered his perspective on what he thought was best for his valued apprentice. Corliss reminded Amos that he had taught him everything he knew and that it might well be time for him to spread his wings and take on new challenges.

A broad smile crossed Corliss's face.

"Amos, you are at the threshold of opportunity. It's not luck that has placed this situation at your doorstep, but the years of preparation you have paid close attention to. Any experienced business owner would easily recognize your talent and potential!"

Amos had also taken reality into account. Although many considered Amos to be Corliss' protégé, several other members of the Corliss family were actively involved in the business. They, in all likelihood, would succeed in running the business at such a time as the sixty-five-year-old founder of the company stepped down.

A month later, Amos returned to the Savage Mine, and on a cool fall day in September 1882, the new Corliss engine was fired up in the Hoist House at the Savage Mine.

Mackay and Amos stood outside. They listened to it build up steam and watched the hoist mechanism shift into operation as the operator engaged the works, engaging the hoist with the Corliss engine.

As it started to work, the Corliss engine began producing a loud rhythmic "chuffing" sound as its large valves opened and closed, regulating the flow of steam to the drive cylinder.

As the first loaded cage, containing cars heavily laden with rich silver ore, began its upward trip to the surface, the smooth and steady beat of the engine brought a broad smile and look of satisfaction to the faces of Mackay and Amos. It was, after all, a testimonial to the months of thought and work that had been completed.

For them, this was a musical symphony to their ears. It meant a job well done, and both men looked pleased.

Mackay extended his hand and asked Amos, "Have you considered the proposition I offered you?"

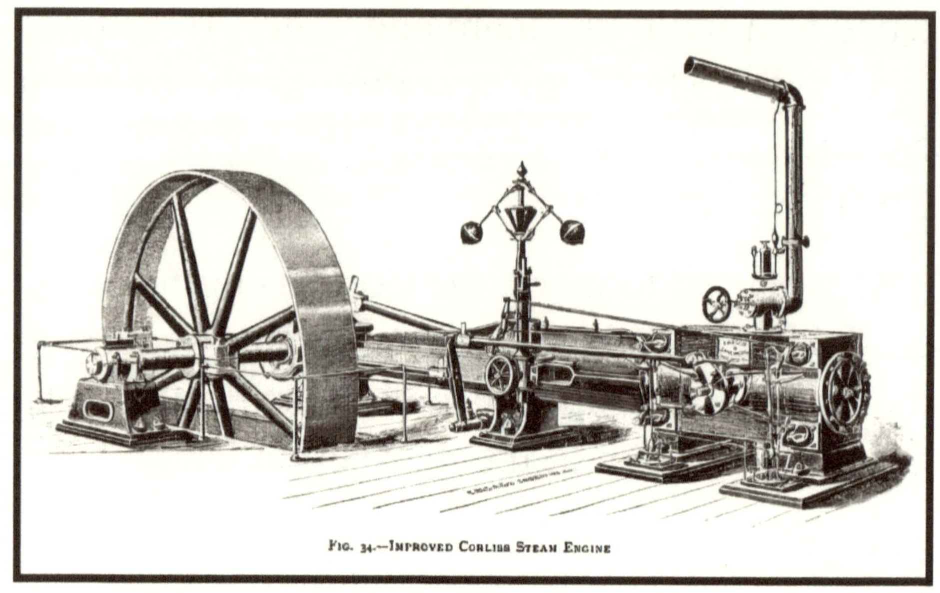

CORLISS ENGINE USED AT THE SAVAGE MINE

Indeed, he had. Amos had spent the past several weeks considering the generous offer Mackay had extended to him upon his return from headquarters back east. There was a lot that Amos had taken under consideration.

The entrepreneurial Spirit of the West had created excitement in his heart. He saw energy and enthusiasm in Mackay, and the men he had been introduced to that were taming a new wilderness, building a bold new direction, and taking more daring risks while coping with and overcoming unpredictable geology, irregular weather patterns, rugged terrain, and the challenges of building infrastructure in a largely undeveloped region.

While Amos had deep respect and admiration for Mister Corliss and was profoundly grateful for his growth and development, he was looking for some excitement in his life that he was not finding back East. And he had Mister Corliss' blessing to pursue his dream.

It had not been an easy decision for Amos by any stretch of the imagination. The two men had many similarities.

George Corliss was indeed a gifted and talented engineer, active in philanthropic and social causes, and a jovial and pleasant individual to be around. He had earned the respect and admiration of the engineering and manufacturing world and actively promoted important social causes of the day.

Likewise, John Mackay was tenacious, intelligent, had extraordinary business savvy, and was widely recognized for his generosity and philanthropy.

On the other hand, Mackay, who had invited Amos to consider leaving his current employer, had big plans for Amos based upon watching him in action.

Amos reached deep into his vest pocket and retrieved the same silver dollar he had pulled out the first time he and Mackay met.

"Remember the first time we met? You put your trust in me."

Flipping the coin high in the air, he extended his hand to Mackay, saying,

"And I won't let you down in our new deal either."

AMOS' SILVER DOLLAR

A MAN WORTH HIS SALT

IN THE days of the Roman Empire, salt was valuable and Roman soldiers were sometimes paid in salt. If a soldier was "worth his salt," it meant he was doing a good job and earning his pay.

This is a story about another fellow whom history has largely overlooked, who was doing a good job and earning his pay.

His name was John Norton. He was an unusual fellow who worked at an underground salt mine in Wyoming County, New York, in the mid-1800s.

John wasn't a miner in the traditional sense. He possessed an unusual ability to locate new veins of salt. He would often be called upon to go into the underground mine alone and use a small wooden tool to tap the mine walls, listening for the sound of salt.

When he heard a promising sound, he would mark the spot with chalk and then return with a drilling team to excavate the salt.

John wasn't the only person able to do that, although individuals with that gift were few in number. People that did what he did were called salt prospectors or "salt boilers."

Salt prospectors like John played an important role in the early days of salt mining when the deposits were not well mapped or understood.

John understood that he was responsible for finding new salt deposits by using his expertise to identify the areas where salt was most likely to be found.

In addition to the wooden tap, John used hammers and chisels to excavate salt from the mine walls. But his favorite tool was the small wooden tool he used to tap the walls and listen for the distinctive sound of salt his trained hearing could pick up.

It wasn't a "walk in the park" kind of job. Salt prospecting was difficult and dangerous, as John had to work in cramped and often unstable underground conditions.

The salt deposits in Wyoming County, New York, in the 1840's were well known. In fact, Native Americans in the area had been using salt springs in the region for centuries before the arrival of European settlers. The Natives discovered that salt allowed them to store food for long periods without spoiling. The preservation of meat and fish was essential during winter when hunting and fishing were less abundant.

In addition to its use in food preservation, salt was also used in Native religious ceremonies and as a trade item. Salt was also believed to have healing properties and was used in medicinal practices.

The first commercial salt works in Wyoming County were established in 1817, and by the

1840's, there were multiple salt works in operation.

John's employer, the Genesee Salt Company, had purchased an earlier operation to take advantage of the presence of salt in the area.

Even though the area was known to have salt, locating specific salt deposits within the larger salt bed that ran throughout the County was still challenging.

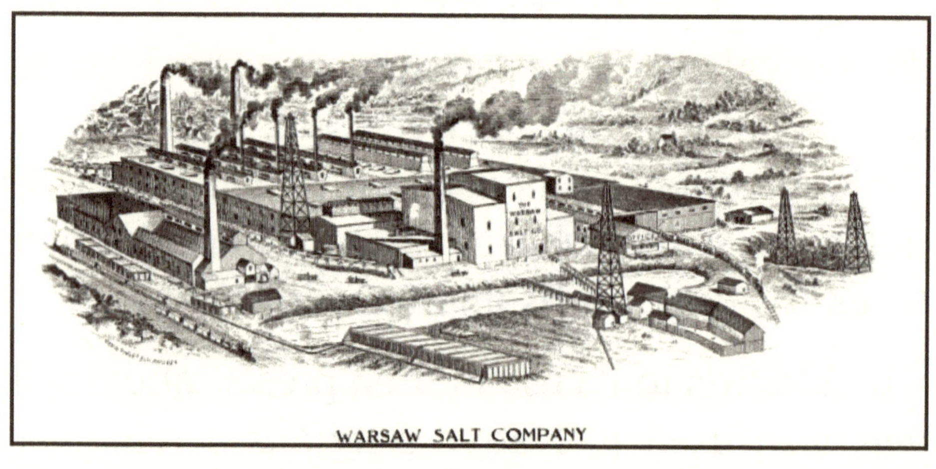

SALT WORKS OF THE WARSAW SALT COMPANY

In some cases, the mining companies in the area relied upon surface indications such as brine seepages to help identify areas that were thought to have higher salt content. Still, the more difficult task of determining the actual location and extent of subterranean salt deposits was done by trial and error.

Common was the practice of sinking exploratory shafts and drilling test holes to determine the quality and quantity of salt that might be present beneath the surface.

Yet, the Company felt the investment was worth it. In the nineteenth century, demand for salt was high, and many entrepreneurs were eager to invest in the development of salt works in the region. As new salt deposits were continually being discovered and exploited, Warsaw, in the middle of Wyoming County, remained an important center of salt production well into the twentieth century.

Salt was in high demand in the mid-19th century in Western New York for several reasons. One of the primary reasons was the growth of the region's agricultural industry, which required large quantities of salt for preserving and processing food products such as meat, dairy, and produce.

The demand for salt also grew as the population of the United States increased and people began to consume more processed and preserved foods.

In addition to its use in food preservation, salt was also utilized in various other industries, including tanning, dyeing, and soap-making. Salt was used to produce chemicals such as chlorine, which was used in a wide range of industrial processes.

The salt deposits in Western New York were particularly valuable because they were located near major transportation routes such as the Erie Canal, making transporting salt to markets throughout the United States relatively easy. This, in turn, helped to spur the growth of the region's salt mining industry and contributed to the high demand for salt during the mid-19th century.

John's talent for finding productive veins of salt was so valuable to the mine's owner that he was paid an extra two dollars per week on top of his regular wages of five dollars per week.

This talent made him a bit of a local celebrity, and it was not uncommon for people in town to stop by the mine to see him at work.

However, John's life took a tragic turn when he became ill with consumption (tuberculosis). Despite his illness, he continued to work in the mine, determined to earn enough money to support his wife and children.

One day, while working alone in the mine, John's illness overtook him, and he collapsed. When he failed to return to the surface, his co-workers went looking for him and found him unconscious in a remote part of the mine. They managed to get him out of the mine and took him to his home, where he died a few days later at the age of 30. The community mourned his passing, and many attended his funeral to pay their respects to the man widely referred to as "A Good Salt."

The company, recognizing John's significant contributions in the decade he had worked in the mine, acknowledged his significant discoveries and continued to provide his widow a monthly stipend for the remainder of her days.

His legacy, inscribed at the bottom of the simple gravestone made of durable Onondaga Limestone, was "John Proved Day after Day that He Was a Man Truly Worth His Salt."

LOADING MINES SALT ORE

A STRIKING IMPRESSION

WHEN ONE thinks of cities which inspired the writers of the 1850's to 1950's, places like New York City, Boston, Chicago, New Orleans, San Francisco, Los Angeles, Salem, Concord, St. Louis, Washington D.C., and Philadelphia come to mind. Few would imagine that a man from the small town of Ishpeming, located on the Upper Peninsula of Michigan, would influence some of the most significant literary works of the twentieth century.

Ishpeming, Michigan, founded in 1862, came into being due to the discovery of significant iron ore deposits. But the story begins with a physician in Oak Park, Illinois, whose patients fondly referred to him as Doctor Clarence. The doctor specialized in ear, nose, and throat (ENT) conditions and served as the Medical Director of the Oak Park Hospital.

He very much enjoyed the outdoors and in 1901 purchased a property on Walloon Lake in northern Michigan and built a cottage where his family could spend their summers, escaping the city's heat.

This lake was large, clear and deep, surrounded by forests and rolling hills. The family found it an ideal location for swimming, boating, fishing and other outdoor activities. Doctor Clarence was an avid outdoorsman and passed his love of hunting and fishing to his children.

His first son was the most enamored by his father's activities and would frequently be at his father's side exploring the bountiful nature of Walloon Lake. His other children enjoyed the swimming and boating activities but they wanted to be back in Oak Park with their friends.

Inspired by his Walloon Lake experiences, the son began writing in high school, capturing and recording those memorable summers on the Upper Peninsula. His teachers recognized his powerful and descriptive writing style and worked with him to develop this gift. That gift got him his first job in journalism immediately following his graduation in 1917.

His writing samples and teacher recommendations helped this bright young man land a job as a reporter for the Kansas City Star newspaper. His editor appreciated his writing style which featured short, declarative sentences and a focus on concrete details and sensory impressions. Unlike many candidates for this position, his writing avoided flowery or ornate language and used simple, direct language to convey his message. This impressed his new boss.

Two years later, he took a job as a correspondent for the Toronto Star newspaper. In 1923 he was sent to cover a major labor strike by iron miners employed by the Cleveland Cliffs Mining Company in Michigan's Upper Peninsula. His familiarity with the Upper Peninsula significantly influenced this decision, enabling him to get this post over the Star's more seasoned correspondents.

With the new assignment in hand, he set up shop in a small community near Ishpeming, which gave him easy access to the striking employees living in the towns and villages near the company's mines. During this two-month assignment, from late July to early September, he used every opportunity to observe and record the miners' daily lives and experience the significant tensions between management and labor. His experiences during this strike he took to heart, which would later form the basis for a novel he would write entitled "In Our Time."

CLEVELAND CLIFFS MINE

With the natural behavior of a local, he visited miners in their homes, frequented local bars and cafes and visited the mines and witnessed first-hand the harsh and dangerous working conditions the miners were forced to endure and the draconian measures the company was using to break the miners' wills. His detailed accounts captured the human struggles of the miners and their families and their desperate efforts to secure fair wages and better working conditions.

The short but intense time spent with the miners and their families in the Upper Peninsula etched into his mind an image he would recall later in his career. He could identify his life as a struggling young writer with these kind, hard-working folks. Later in his life, his memoir, "A Moveable Feast," would showcase his struggle in this work published after his death.

Those two months covering the Cleveland Cliffs Mining Company strike had one of the most significant impacts on his career. His distinctive writing style, honed during this time, has been given the name "Hemingwayesque," a style of writing that allows the reader to draw their own conclusions about the characters and events in his stories,

ERNEST HEMINGWAY

And all who have read Ernest Hemingway's works can attest to his emotional dimensions and impact. In his novel, "In Our Time," Ernest created a character named Nick Adams based on his own real experiences while working on the strike assignment.

Following the Cleveland Cliffs Mining Company strike, Ernest Hemingway, the young and talented reporter, began writing what would become a collection of twenty-four "Nick Adams Stories." In this collection, he used the Nick Adams character to depict his own life experiences and his fondness for and connection to the natural world, which had its roots on Walloon Lake.

Ernest Hemingway's personal experiences in Ishpeming also inspired him to write several other works, including "The Old Man and the Sea," which tells the story of an aging fisherman who, like the miners in Ishpeming, had to rely on his strength and determination to survive.

In many ways, our lives can be helpful to us. Hemingway's works reflected upon his vast and varied life experiences in such a way to portray the issues that continue to challenge society today, coping with loss, struggle, and redemption.

ALL I WANTED WAS TO SEE A SUNRISE

IT WAS a chilly late November morning in southeastern Pennsylvania, and at three O'clock in the morning, Alvin was gently awakened by his mother.

"Alvin, it's time to get ready for work."

The ten-year-old lad with pasty white skin threw back the threadbare cover under which he had huddled, swung his feet over the side of his tiny bed and reached for the worn overalls on the bedpost with one hand while trying to rub the sleep from his eyes with the other.

He had had such a pleasant dream. Such a shame it had to end.

"Brrr!" He murmured as his feet hit the cold floor, "That did the trick. Now I'm awake ready to start a new day."

His tiny feet padded down the worn, narrow wooden stairs into the slightly warmer kitchen, where the warmth of the coal-fed stove took the chill off the room.

He went to the porcelain wash basin on the side table, splashing cold water into his face.

"Now I'm fully awake!" He said to himself.

His colorful dream of minutes ago flashed back into his mind. In his imagination, he saw a large yellow and orange ball coming up over the eastern mountains and as it reached higher into the sky, it began to warm the tree-covered hillsides, and then the meadows with cattle and livestock milled about the pasture.

"There's no time for daydreaming, Alvin; you'll be late for your shift!" his mother scolded.

Pulling back the maple stool, he watched her

place a steaming bowl of oatmeal in front of him. He gobbled it down. He attached a set of heavy leather kneepads to his coveralls and put on his shoes with reinforced leather soles.

"OK, work uniform ready," He said to himself.

Now, to get to the hoist house of the mine before the five O'clock whistle when the first cage of coal miners was lowered into the pitch-black depth of the underworld. He had to be in place and ready with the first men and mine cars coming through the narrow tunnel.

Alvin was just one of a small army of children that, in the 1870's, were found working in the coal mines of the day.

Some, like Alvin, were "trapper boys" whose sole job was to open and close the heavy ventilation doors known as "traps" which were used to regulate airflow through the mine. The trap doors are used to direct the currents of air through the different sections of the mine.

Young children working in the mines in 1870

was common. Other boys his age, considered smaller and weaker, were employed tending switches or coupling the coal shuttle cars. The stronger children were given jobs working with the other miners, picking out coal and loading lumps of extracted coal into cars.

Alvin had gotten this job due to his family's circumstances. Deeply indebted to the Company Store, Alvin's mother had pleaded with the Company official for a job for her son.

"He is twelve years old and will be a good worker; I promise!" she had said, with tears in her eyes.

After recently losing her husband in a mine explosion, she knew she was totally dependent upon the Company to provide a way for her to support her son Alvin and four-year-old daughter. Alvin taking a job in the mine offered the only way to avoid destitution.

So Alvin knew his job was necessary to sustain his mother and sister and was resigned to begin another day of the same.

Alvin had been assigned to a specific trap door. He dreaded this part, crawling on his hands and knees through a series of narrow tunnels to reach the chamber where he was stationed. The access tunnels were just wide enough for a small boy to crawl through; some were several hundred feet long. He was glad that his mother had sewn the heavy leather patches on the knees of his coveralls. Unlike the miners who wore work clothes, protective equipment, and helmets with headlamps, Alvin and the other trapper boys wore regular clothing and had no special protective gear. They sat day in and day out in total darkness.

The third access tunnel he squirmed through finally brought him to the small, cramped chamber cut out of the coal seam next to his assigned door. This was his workstation for the next ten hours, located next to the heavy trap door he was responsible for operating.

This tiny chamber carved out of the rock had no light, and there was no ventilation other than the airflow of the tunnel he was in. Fortunately, there was a board for him to sit on, for which he was grateful as that tunnel was continually dripping water.

TRAPPER BOY AT HIS DOOR

Alvin felt fortunate. At least he had room to sit. Some of the chambers were so small that the boys he knew had to sit with their knees bent up to their chests.

His job was simple but very important. Opening the trap door to which he had been assigned involved pulling the heavy hemp rope tied to the trap door at one end and running up through a pulley on the tunnel ceiling. Alvin held the other end of the rope. The trap door would remain closed at all times and only open on two occasions.

When a miner needed to come through, they would typically call out to Alvin to let him know they needed to pass through his trap door. Alvin would then pull on the rope to raise the door to allow the miners to pass through. After they had passed, he would release the rope allowing the door to close. Alvin understood that he had to be careful not to let the rope become tangled or snagged while operating the trap door, as this could cause it to break or become damaged.

There were times when the air quality in the mine became stale or dangerous. When this happened, a foreman or safety inspector told Alvin to open his trap door to allow more air to circulate.

An underground mine is a complex system of airflow to circulate air in the tunnels. This is necessary to provide air for the miners, and reduce the buildup of toxic and explosive gases in the mine. Trap Doors and "Stoppings" were two of the most important underground elements.

There were "stoppings", strong walls that were built underground to divide the mine into different areas and constructed to help control the flow of air to keep the miners safe and make their work easier. The construction and maintenance of stoppings in mine ventilation were usually performed by skilled miners or mine ventilation engineers. These individuals had the knowledge and expertise to design and install stoppings in a way that facilitated proper airflow and ensured the safety and effectiveness of the ventilation system.

The trap-door boys like Alvin, did the other part, operating the trap doors (or gates) in the underground passages. Their primary responsibility was to open and close these doors as needed.

Stoppings, on the other hand, were barriers or

partitions constructed within the mine passages to control the flow of air and direct it to specific areas of the mine. They were essential components of the ever expanding mine ventilation system. Stoppings helped to prevent the spread of harmful gases, control air currents, and ensure that fresh air reached the areas where miners were working.

While the trap-door boys like Alvin were not directly involved in constructing or maintaining stoppings, their role in regulating the movement of carts and traffic within the mine was crucial for the effectiveness of the ventilation system. By opening and closing trap doors at the right times, Alvin understood he played an important role in maintaining proper air circulation and preventing the buildup of dangerous gases in certain areas of the mine.

Alvin took his job very seriously. He knew he needed to be attentive and responsive at all times, as changes in air quality in the mine could happen quickly and unexpectedly. He constantly remained on the lookout for signals and calls from other workers in the mine and was ready to open and close his trap door as needed to maintain a safe and healthy working environment for everyone.

Within a week of starting this job, Alvin realized that monotony was the trapper boy's constant enemy. Sitting in the dark for hours at a time invited thoughts of sleep or becoming distracted from the job. Alvin chose to occupy his mind with daydreams, fantasies, and imagining himself in other places. While some of the trapper boys said they passed the time by singing or whistling tunes to themselves, Alvin didn't want to do this as he knew he needed to listen carefully for the next time his door needed to be pulled open.

What kept Alvin focused was his mother reminding him how important this job was.

"Alvin, those doors help prevent mine explosions. It was a 'black damp' explosion in that same mine that took the life of your Father, you know!"

Alvin was only eight when it had happened, but he remembered the spectacle.

The siren at the Breaker had gone off mid-day, and all in the camp came running. The siren only sounded at the beginning and end of the shift unless something terrible had happened. Over the next four hours, the women and children had huddled together as miners recovered and brought out the bodies of their colleagues that had died in the massive underground explosion.

That was the only recent memory of daylight that remained in Alvin's imagination, and it was a very unpleasant one. Unlike that dark rainy afternoon, he longed to see a sunrise. That's why he began crafting a more vibrant and colorful dream.

"Someday," he thought as he sat on his hewn perch, "Someday, I'll be able to see a sunrise."

And those hopes kept him going day after day and month after month. His meager pay was enough to keep his mother and sister housed and fed. He felt really good about that!

With each hour of his twelve-hour shift passing, he listened for a shout, the kick of a boot on his heavy door, or the sound of approaching mine cars screeching against the steel rails of the passage floor. And after opening, he provided safe passage of workers and materials, carefully closing his door each time. Exhausted at the end of the shift, he crawled back through the access tunnels to the main shaft and climbed into the cage with several other miners. A bell clanged and the cage slowly ascended to the top, a trip of more than twelve hundred vertical feet. Once reaching the upper world, he began his trek to the small miner's shack on the hillside, ignoring a world he was too tired to enjoy.

You can imagine how hard it is for a young boy to pass these twelve hours daily, sitting in total darkness, alone, in a silent, damp passage.

Occasionally his mind would wander as infrequent gaps between door openings overcame his spirit. The stupefying, brutalizing tedium of doing nothing was becoming agonizing to him.

He now was thinking BIG! Not only his hope of experiencing a sunrise but also to attend school.

At Sunday school, Alvin had discovered that other children his age knew their letters, and some were learning how to write. But as this mining camp had no school, education fell to the mother, who may have had some formal education. Alvin's mother had not had this opportunity.

Still, he fought to keep the dream alive. "Someday, I will see a sunrise."

Two years later, Alvin, now twelve, had learned that there were jobs "topside" in the Coal Breaker.

Some boys he had met at Sunday school had told him about this, and he found it so exciting.

It sounded like the kind of day where he could actually experience a Sunrise!

He was familiar with the coal breaker, a large coal processing plant at the main part of the mine which breaks coal into various useful sizes. The Breaker Boys sat on wooden benches on a steep slope perched over the coal chutes and conveyor belts.

TYPICAL COAL BREAKER BUILDING

Huge conveyers lifted coal from the mine to the top of the Breaker building, where the Breaker Boys would sit with their quick and nimble fingers picking through the descending coal to remove slate and other impurities in the coal.

It was a continuous and dangerous job, removing this often-sharp debris from the coal before it went down into the crusher and sorting machines beneath them.

BREAKER BOYS AT WORK

But what Alvin heard was that it was an above-ground job, and the pay was considerably better. A "breaker boy" could earn as much as one dollar for two weeks of work, which would greatly help his family.

Since he had been at his post opening trap doors without incident for two years, he had gotten to know Clark, his Section Boss, quite well, and when he inquired about getting a job in the Breaker, his Section Boss said he'd be happy to recommend him.

A few days later, early in the shift, Clark, his Section Boss, came back to say Alvin had been approved to take a job in the Breaker. With joy in his heart, he couldn't wait to tell his mother at the end of his shift.

But that was not to be.

At about nine O'clock in the morning, a massive blast occurred on his level. Alvin was in the process of opening his trap door for an oncoming ore car, and the blast slammed his small body against the wall of the tunnel behind the heavy wooden door he had tended for the past two years.

In the next section, another Trapper Boy had fallen asleep at his post, leaving his assigned wide door open. The ventilation airflow was interrupted, and a pocket of deadly and explosive "black damp" methane gas had collected. A spark from a mine car's wheels set off the explosion.

As the mine rescue crews pored through the rubble and debris, they passed Alvin's door several times, each time evaluating dead or wounded miners.

Clark, the Section Boss, had been spared, and as he searched each tunnel, he spied Alvin's heavy wooden door that had been blown off its hinges and a tiny leg sticking out beneath it.

The mine rescue crew quickly worked to lift the hundred-pound door from the young Trapper.

Alvin was still breathing, and his crushed body was loaded atop a coal car and quickly taken to the surface.

As the mine car carrying his young form reached the surface, he was lifted gently off the car onto a stretcher to be taken to a nearby hospital tent set up to treat the injured.

As he was transported to the tent, the bright morning sunlight shone down upon his face. A smile appeared on his bruised and bloody lips.

"It is such a beautiful thing!" he thought, ignoring the pain coursing through his tiny damaged body,

The stretcher attendants missed it, as it only lasted an instant.

His final thought brought him great peace before his spirit joined his father's.

"I am so glad I finally got to see a sunrise."

PEARL THE MINE MULE

MY NAME is Pearl.

I'm a mule, a "mare" mule, to be more precise.

I was born in a beautiful mule farm in Western Ohio in 1899.

The older mules told me that I was destined to be some kind of special. The mule is a hybrid animal having a jackass, commonly called a jack, for a sire and a mare for a dam. My father was a strong male donkey apparently who I always remember being referred to as "Jack" but my mother was referred to as a well-bred a female horse named Daisy. I vaguely remember my mother and what our time was like after I arrived in the world.

My first month was primarily focused on bonding with my mother, learning to stand and gaining strength in my wobbly legs. I remember mostly the wonderful time nursing and sleeping. I recall exploring my surroundings within the safety of mother's presence. She explained to me the sights, sounds, and smells of the world. Mother's gentle voice was beautiful to my young ears and he had a distinctive scent. Mother watched over me with a understanding gaze, and watched me clumsily wobble around in my stall.

Shortly after I began to gain better control over my body and started to practice walking, trotting, and running. I remember mother inviting me to play with the other young mules in the paddock, often engaging in friendly bouts of "mock" fighting with my new friends.

I started to get what mother called "teeth" and I learned how to begin nibbling on solid food, such as grass and hay. Mother sometimes was startled when I was nursing. Perhaps it was my new teeth? I was starting to get excited about independently exploring my environment.

By my third month I could see I was growing and my legs were becoming stronger and more stable, and I was able to trot and gallop with the other older mules. For the first time I felt comfortable being more adventurous, venturing away from mother for short periods to explore my surroundings.

It was then that I found it fun to interact with other horses, farm animals, and even humans.

By this time, I had a nice set of strong teeth and mother moved me from her delicious mother's milk to a diet primarily consisting of forage and other solid foods.

Mother began to teach me basic behaviors and manners through observation and gentle correction her and other herd members.

I was taken away from my mother after about three months, but she told me that I was going to grow up to be strong and special. After I stopped nursing and was separated from my mother, I was put in a special part of the barn with other mares.

We mares got to basic training before the male "jack" mules. By the time I was six months old I had been halter-broken, could be lead, and enjoyed my daily grooming. I understand that the jack mules were more stubborn and difficult.

Us "girls" thought that they looked a bit foolish for the trouble they were giving their handlers.

The first three years of my life felt pretty special to me as well. The people at the mule farm were very good to me.

Every day I ate a tasty diet that includes hay, and grain, and a handler would take me out in the paddock so I could get used to human contact and develop good manners. Manners are important you know. Some days I would be let into a corral where my handlers introduced me to other mules and horses and watched how I behaved around them. I was always polite and got along well with all of them.

The best part of my days is when they let me out in the big green pasture where I could exercise and play with other mules.

LIFE AT THE MULE FARM

But I didn't spend all day frolicking and playing. I liked to examine pasture, closely examining the fence and the gates, looking for interesting details, and trying to learn what lay beyond the fences.

But after doing this for more than two years, I

was feeling like I was ready for something bigger, better.

I thought "Is this all there is?"

Yes, I was beginning to tire of the same daily routine.

I would so much enjoy doing something new and different!

Then one day, I saw a group of men that were standing on the edge of the pasture. They were pointing at me, and some of the other mules grazing and playing in the pasture.

They weren't the men from the farm.

"Who are these men?" I wondered, "What are they looking for?"

And these same men showed up, looking at us mules for the next two days. Some of these men wore work clothes and had soiled boots. There was one that seemed to be paying particular attention to me. I moved a bit closer to check him out.

He wore sturdy boots, and heavy work pants, a

long-sleeved shirt, and a hat for protection from the sun, and carried a notebook and seemed to be taking notes as he evaluated us mules. Later in the day they were joined by an older man wearing pressed pants and a clean long-sleeved canvas shirt. This well-dressed man began talking with some of the other men, pointing at the various mules in the paddock. After a while, the group of men left.

"I wonder what that was all about?" I thought to myself.

The following morning, there was a great commotion as the stable hands moved the mules in the pasture to a much smaller corral. One by one, each mule was led out into the paddock where there was this group of men seated on wooden benches.

The older man with a large-brimmed white hat and a powerful voice appeared in the center of the corral, and as each mule was led out by its halter, he would stand next to the mule and begin to talk about each mule.

I found this most peculiar behavior.

"What in the world is going on here?" I wondered.

When the man with the white hat was talking, the men on the bench would get very loud, throwing up their hands and yelling loudly, often yelling on top of each other.

Then the man with the white hat would yell "SOLD!" and the commotion would die down. That mule would then be led away, another one would take its place, and the whole process would be repeated.

I must admit, this was most confusing.

What I found most interesting was fewer hands were raised in the group when a "Jack Mule" was brought forward. These male mules didn't like this at all and made it difficult for the stable hand to get these mules into the center of the corral. Unlike us girls, the male mules were very agitated and quite headstrong. The more rambunctious these mules behaved, the fewer the hands the men raised. And with some of

these mules, no hands of the men on the bleach-
ers were raised at all.

It made me think, "Apparently, I'm not supposed to act like that!"

And so, when it was my turn to be led into the
center, I calmly and confidently followed my
handler into the center of the paddock, taking
steady and confident steps with my head held
high.

This is *my* day to impress these people.

And apparently, I did. As the man with the
white hat spoke about me, dozens of hands went
up, and the shouting and hand raising went on
for several minutes.

So I had won some kind of popularity contest!

When I got led back to the corral, my friend
Maude came over to me.

"You looked real good out there! Your new
owner really liked you," she said.

"New owner?" I asked, "What do you mean?

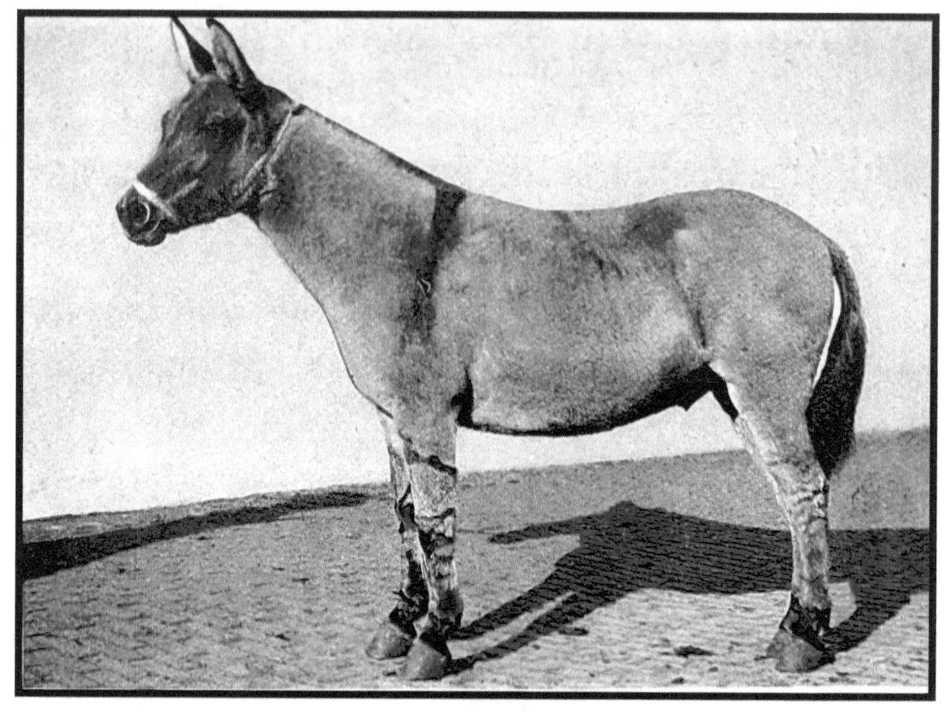

PEARL AT TWO YEARS OLD

Maude, who was almost a year older than me and had far more experience, had been through two of these and explained what had just happened. Here's what she told me:

"Held twice a year, this was an important event in those parts where mule and workhorse breeders advertised their animals in the newspapers and trade magazines, their strongest and healthiest that were deemed ready to work," she explained.

"The buyers looking at us today have come from many different places and need good mules for various tasks.

SALE AT THE MULE FARM

"Farmers look for strong draft animals on farms, particularly in the South, where they are preferred over horses for our strength, endurance, and ability to work in hot and humid conditions. Mine mules are preferred in coal mines to pull carts of coal and equipment through the tunnels over pit ponies due to our strength, surefootedness, and ability to navigate the narrow and often steep tunnels.

"Men from all over come to this farm to find

and purchase mules for their particular needs. Some of the mules that have been sold were needed to pull wagons. Loggers and others in the timber industry also have come here to buy strong, sure-footed mules to haul logs out of the forest and transport them to sawmills. I've even seen mules that were sold to work on construction sites to haul heavy materials like bricks, stones, and timbers."

I had no idea that there were so many kinds of things we mules could do!

Maude continued:

"Many of the young 'Jack' mule colts that have been sold went for less than $200. The new owners that hoped they'd get a good strong mule better realize that they will have to break them in first. As we know, they're pretty stubborn boys. They sure have their work cut out for them."

While Maude was explaining this to me, two men came up to me. One was a handler from the farm, but I didn't recognize the other man.

Then I recall, this man was the one who was at the pasture the previous day, taking notes and pointing at me.

Maude nuzzled up to me, and said, "I think he just bought you!"

And she was right. The farm hand opened the corral and led me out and gave the lead to the other man, who he called "Pete" who led me out of the farm, down a road that led away from the farm to a place where there was a strange looking device.

I had never seen anything like it on the farm. It looked like a long, rectangular-shaped box made of wood and steel that had with a sloping roof and two doors on each end. The walls of the box appeared to have been made of wooden slats with gaps in between.

I had seen something like this at the farm that was used for the chickens at the mule farm. One of the side doors was open and a wooden ramp led up to the opening from the ground. The man called "Pete" slowly led me up the ramp. When

I got inside, I looked around. It was a little bit like my stable back at the farm. There were several stalls like we had at the farm, with wood walls and "Pete" led me into one of these, closed the gate, and showed me that there was a trough filled with water and a bucket that had some hay to eat.

RAILROAD STOCK CAR

I had seen something like this at the farm that was used for the chickens at the mule farm. One of the side doors was open and a wooden ramp led up to the opening from the ground. The man called "Pete" slowly led me up the ramp. When I got inside, I looked around. It was a little bit like my stable back at the farm. There were several stalls like we had at the farm, with wood walls and "Pete" led me into one of these, closed the gate, and showed me that there was a trough filled with water and a bucket that had some hay to eat.

As I got used to these new surroundings, two other mules from the farm were brought in by different men and put into their own stalls. Then all three of the men left, and the door to this strange "stable" was closed.

After a few minutes, there was a loud clanking sound and I could feel a shudder and this strange room begin to move. I couldn't see outside because unlike my stable I couldn't see outside because there were no windows, only the little bit of light I could see through the wooden slats. Then I heard a screech and a whistle. Those were familiar sounds. I had seen a strange kind of wagon train of sorts way passing beyond our farm.

So this WAS a new experience! I'm part of this "wagon train" and don't have to pull it!

How much fun this will be!

I quickly got used to the sound of the train moving along the tracks, and could feel the floor shaking beneath my feet. Even though the air is dusty and smells like hay and is a bit hot and stuffy, I felt safe because there isn't enough space for me to move about.

I like new experiences. I hope this train is taking me someplace where I can run around and play outside again.

Over the following three days, the train pulling this car started and stopped several times, and sometimes animals were brought on or taken off. But I always had fresh hay and water.

I wondered, "Where are the others going?"

By this time, I was an "old hat" at this riding in this strange stable and used to this bumpy and noisy journey. Unlike some of the other animals on board who were frightened by the train's sudden movements and loud noises, I was not affected at all. I'm pretty special that way.

Finally, train came to a stop and the side door was once again opened, and there was Pete who carefully unloaded me.

"What is this?" I wondered. I was taken aback. There was no grass, only rocky ground and piles of black coal mine tailings.

I was in shock!

It wasn't just the sight in front of me, but my keen sense of smell immediately picked up several strange and pungent scents. There was a dust that seemed to hang in the air, a fine black powder that had a distinct earthy and smoky odor. I also was aware of smoke and soot that filled the air. Not the clean fresh air I knew back at the farm, but an acrid aroma of smoke that smelled like rotten eggs.

Not all of these smells were unpleasant or unfamiliar to me. I picked up the smell of freshly cut timber a natural and woody aroma like the new posts and barns on the farm that mixed with the other scents present. There was also odor of animals, including the smell of manure and hay used for feeding them. That made me feel a bit better.

It must have been obvious to Pete. He saw my ears pinned back, my wide eyes, and how I was shaking.

Pete could see what was happening and he held onto my halter and came over and spoke gently into my ear, just as he had done when he put me on that train. His calm voice reassured me.

"So this is where you'll begin your life as a mine mule," he exclaimed. "Dahlin', don't you worry. I'll take good care of you."

Hearing Pete's calming voice, my moment of anxiety passed, but still, a doubt remained.

"I want to do something new and different, but I don't know about this!" I thought.

Little did I know that my willingness to learn new things and adapt to new surroundings was about to be put to the test.

The following morning, Pete showed up,

brushed me and led me outside the barn where I had enjoyed my first good rest in several days.

As I scanned the surrounding landscape, I was aghast!

"This looks nothing like the farm where I was born." I thought.

And indeed, it was not. There were no grassy pastures, rolling hills, or brightly painted barns.

Instead, I found myself standing directly in front of the Shenandoah #7 coal mine.

Pete took his time, walked me around the area and explained to me what each building was.

He began by showing me a lump of coal. I had no idea what it was, and didn't look like something that would be good to eat.

"This is Coal," he said, "It is made from plants that lived a long time ago. It is found in the ground and is used to make heat. This is what we do here. The coal miners find coal and it will be your job to help get it to the surface."

So now I had my first idea of what I would be doing. I had an important job!

Pete knew I had no clue about what was going on here so he explained each building.

"That tall structure built over the mine shaft supports the hoisting machinery used to bring coal, men and equipment to the surface.

"Next to this is the engine house, where the steam engine inside is used to power the hoist and pumps for the mine.

"Nearby, over by the railroad tracks, is the coal breaker that is used to sort, clean, and size the coal. And those are conveyors and chutes that take the coal to awaiting railroad hopper cars beneath the structure."

To my left were several smaller buildings. Pete led me past these smaller buildings, explaining which one was an office, storage shed, or repair shop as they went.

This certainly is different!

The tranquil pasture where I had been raised

had been replaced by this busy, noisy, dusty, and bustling place, with no vegetation visible anywhere, no trees for shade, and no tender grasses upon which to munch.

For that matter where I was now standing didn't even resemble a field, but instead an ugly valley full of slimy pools of black water and surrounded by tall mounds of dark, menacing black rock.

Nervously, I turned my head this way and that way hoping to see tree-covered hills, but even the hillsides had the scars of excavation on them.

Naturally, I began to panic.

Back at the mule farm, when I was told fetched the best auction price of the day, I felt so special – like I was to be doing great things. But seeing this for the first time has left me feeling not-so-special after all.

I thought about my stable mates back at the mule farm who had also been sold off to work. I'll bet they're in someplace nice; pulling a plow or hauling timber or a wagon of produce.

I thought I was headed for someplace where my beauty, strength, and intelligence would be put to good use.

Pete, the kindly man who had purchased me at the auction, gently whispered in my ear again, saying, "Dahlin', don't you fret none. We're going to dress you up and send you to school

School?

Getting dressed up and going to school sounded pretty special, although, quite frankly, I didn't know what it meant.

But I'm here now, and I am willing to learn new things and adapt to new surroundings.

Gently, Pete led me to a small building on the edge of the property where several barns existed. He led me into the first one, saying to the man in the leather apron, "Let's get our girl fixed up with some fancy headwear."

The man with the apron started to work, stopping to look me straight on and then taking a few measurements of my head with a tape measure. Then he went back to a cobbler's workbench where he busied himself for a bit, doing I don't know what.

Then he returned with three pieces of soft material he laid across my head and then took them back to his workbench, where he sat on a stool. I began hearing hammering and snipping sounds. Then going to a machine next to his workbench, there were short bursts of rhythmic whirring noise, and finally, he stood up and said, "AHA! That should do it."

Turning back toward me, he held a fancy leather bonnet with double stitches, two holes in the top, and a strap beneath it. As he approached me, I looked at this contraption and thought, this is EXACTLY the kind of special headwear that a special mule like me should wear. He carefully slid the thick leather bonnet over my head, covering most of my head, leaving only my two pretty ears sticking out the top. Cinching the chin strap, he snugged up the cap. I felt really special for the first time since leaving that boxcar.

Pete said to the man, "Nice Job, Alex."

He took my lead and led me to the second barn, which was a stable with stalls similar to what we had back at the mule farm.

As we walked along, Pete explained to me that these bonnets were designed to protect my head from injuries and abrasions that could be caused by low-hanging roofs, sharp rocks or other debris in the mine.

I must admit, it was a pretty fancy piece of headwear.

This IS special!

And knowing that none of my pasture mates back at the farm would have anything like this made this moment even sweeter.

For you see, my leather bonnets were made of heavy leather and were designed to fit snugly over my head, covering my ears, forehead, and top. It was secured with wide straps that fastened under my chin and behind my ears, and Alex lined it with soft sheepskin for added comfort.

I felt like I was wearing a fancy crown! Yes, I was mule royalty!

The barn Pete led me back to, was smaller than what I had at the mule farm, and only had eight stalls. There I got brushed down, my feet washed, and given some fresh water to drink and a feedbag full of tasty oats.

As Pete prepared to leave for the night, he came over and whispered in my ear, "Dahlin', rest up. Tomorrow you're going to Mule school."

As he left, pulling the heavy door of the barn closed, I wondered, "What is Mule school?"

Early the following morning, I found out. As Pete arrived, he brushed me down, led me out of the barn, and up the hillside on a steep but narrow dirt road, headed for the "school," which looked more like a somewhat flat surface, carved out the nearby rocky hillside.

There was an opening in the hillside where several feet below were several ore mine cars. Some were empty, and others were loaded with coal. A man was standing at the top of a chute.

Now if you or I looked at "mule school," it might look like a large model train layout, with a big oval track and two switches, each connecting the oval track to a siding of about thirty feet of straight track.

On this circuit, there was a hopper where a pile of coal got loaded into an empty mine car and a different place where the loaded coal car full of ore was to be dropped off,

Pete and the trainer at Mule School patiently worked with me for the next several days.

On my first day, Pete hooked me up with a "breast harness" so I could learn how to pull the coal mine cars down in the mine. It was to distribute the weight of the multiple mine cars I would be pulling across my chest and shoulders rather than placing all the weight on my neck.

Made with the same craftsmanship as my bonnet, it had a wide leather strap around my chest and straps running down my sides attached to the mine car I would pull. Like my bonnet, it was padded with a soft material to prevent chafing or rubbing, and Pete made sure the straps were adjusted to ensure a snug fit without being too tight or restrictive.

Pete also introduced me to the "back strap" harness that he said would help control the speed and direction of the load I would be pulling. This harness was a leather strap or band fitted around my hindquarters and attached to the mine car. He explained that since many of the tunnels were not level, the "back strap" harness would help to slow down the mine car and prevent it from running into my legs.

Pete was kind and patient as he introduced me to these harnesses and showed me how each worked until he saw I was comfortable with these additions. Once we were done with this step, we proceeded to the next stage of Mule School, which was to teach me how to pull heavy loads safely and efficiently while minimizing the risk of injury or strain.

Next came learning how to navigate obstacles I'd encounter in the mine, such as uneven surfaces, steep inclines, and narrow passageways. Being very sure-footed, this came easy to me. Pete told me that in this mine, there were areas that were particularly steep or had narrow passages that required the mine mules to be particularly nimble and agile.

I was then taken to a large nearby barn that had no windows. Pete told me I needed to learn to be comfortable working in low-light conditions and sometimes in total darkness. Part of this training even included being fitted with special "blinders" to help me see better in the dark.

Next, I had to learn how to respond to commands, and I was trained in responding to various commands from several different people so I would stop, turn, or move forward when told to.

Then back to the track, where I learned how to pick up an empty mine car and how to wait at the coal chute until my mine car was loaded. Starting with one loaded mine car the first day, Pete added another each day, showing me how to pull my loaded mine cars around the track to the siding.

After I had mastered this part of the training, Pete pulled me aside and whispered in my ear.

"Dahlin', this next part may be a bit difficult for you to understand. Just watch what I do, OK?"

Underground mine cars ran on a network of tracks. The Shenandoah #7 mine had an underground track system organized around a series of main haulage ways (large tunnels) that provided access to the different sections of the mine. These main entries were wide enough to allow for the passage of multiple mine cars, and the #7 mine had two parallel tracks to accommodate traffic in both directions. Branching off from the main was a series of "rooms," or "headings," which were smaller tunnels leading to the coal seams being mined. These rooms were narrower than the main entries and had a single track for moving mine cars. In addition to the main entries and rooms, the track system had a series of "crosscuts," which were tunnels that connected different sections of the mine, and "turnouts," junctions where the direction of the track could be changed.

The turnout switches to access these areas could be operated by a mule using a "kick switch." Operating this type of switch was the next stage of my training. Pete took her over and showed her what the switch looked like. It was a section of rail that was moveable, attached to what Pete called a switch stand, and was positioned at a junction where the direction of the track needed to be changed. The switch stand was outside the track, which would ordinarily be the tunnel's wall.

The switch stand had a mechanism triggered by the impact of a mule's hoof. Pete showed me the metal plate that was connected to the switch rail through a linkage system.

First, Pete showed me how it was done and then brought me to the switch to try it myself.

When I stepped on the trigger mechanism,

it activated the linkage system and moved the switch rail to the desired position, enabling changing the direction of the track. I got excited, and with Pete's guidance, I did it several more times and was getting pretty good at it.

Well, doesn't that make me special?

The design of a kick switch was simple and reliable, allowing for quick and efficient switching of tracks with minimal effort on the part of the mule driver. It relied on the natural motion of the mule's gait to activate the switch. By the end of the day, I had completed this part of my training and could throw the switch to get into the siding by kicking the switch points along the track with my hooves.

I even showed off a little bit and made Pete laugh.

I heard Pete and the trainer say, "This is one smart mule," as they were impressed by how quickly I picked this up.

It shouldn't have been a surprise. After all, being so smart, I was intent on proving once again what a fast learner I was.

I spent the next day gathering ore-laden cars from the loading faces of the practice area to the siding off the main track and then returning the empty mine cars on the other siding to the loading chute at what the men called the "working face."

I was committed to making Pete proud of me and paid close attention to each lesson.

As a result of my intelligence and determination, I finished Mule School two days before the typical mule, and I sure hoped that Pete would be proud of me, and it appeared that he was.

After completing my final Mule School lesson, Pete led me back to the stable. He leaned over and whispered in my ear, "Dahlin', you did real good - you've got the rest of the week to rest up, before we take you down into the mine - this is where it gets fun."

I nodded, feeling it was the best way to show Pete it was already fun.

After completing Mule School, I was anxious to discover what was next in her new adventure.

Other than my daily grooming by a stable hand, I didn't see Pete much for the next three days. I felt lonely; after being the center of attention (and star pupil) for the past week. I was also getting quite hungry because my feed bin had not been refilled since I was put here.

How could I have known that for three days before making its journey to the bottom of the mine, the mine operators had learned that a mule should get no food or water? If this was not done, there was a danger of me having a ruptured bladder or suffocation as I was slowly being lowered to the bottom of the mine.

On the third day Pete finally came and again whispered into my ear, "Dahlin', this will be a new experience for you. I need you to trust me. You'll be in a whole new world when this day ends."

Then Pete put on my fancy leather bonnet,

As I was led to the mine entrance where Pete

had told me there was a cage was that miners took to go down in the mine, something strange happened. When we got to the main mine shaft, Pete stopped and put a blindfold on me. I've never been blindfolded before, so this was a new experience. I didn't know whether I should be afraid or wait for a surprise when the blindfold was removed. But I trusted this man, Pete.

I'll assume a big surprise is waiting for me.

But what happened next, I was NOT prepared for.

Apparently, what I learned later is that moving a nine-hundred-pound mule into the bottom of a mine was a significant task. There were only two ways to go about this; a specifically constructed mule cage or hoisting the mule down into the mine using a harness.

The cages used to take the miners down into the mine were too small. It was quite challenging to cram four to six men into one cage for the journey to the bottom of the shaft, let alone get a heavy mule several hundred feet underground.

However, a specially constructed mule cage was heavy, cumbersome, difficult to get the mules into, and meant a significant loss of time getting the cage in and out of the shaft. So, the harness approach was the preferred way to lower mules into the mine.

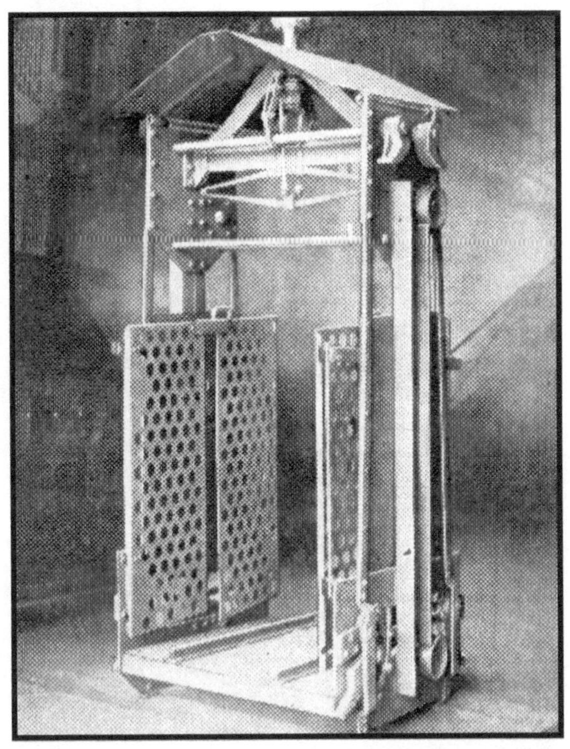

MINE CAGE FOR LOWERING MEN INTO THE MINE

And that was how they intended to lower me into the mine.

The harness itself was a simple affair. The cobbler who crafted my bonnet had already measured me earlier and had constructed a harness specifically for this task using pieces of old canvas and rubber belting that were securely riveted together.

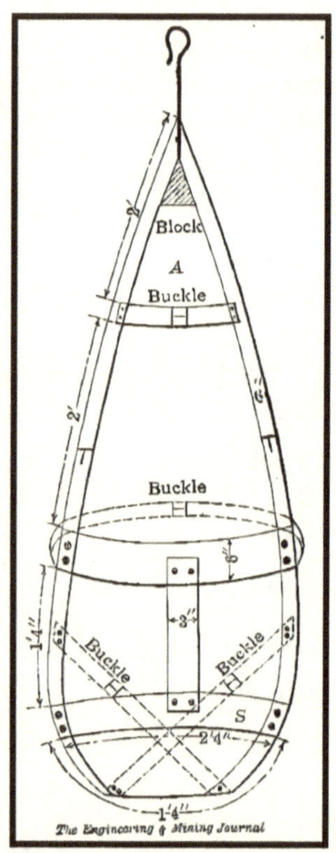

SPECIAL HARNESS MADE FOR LIFTING PEARL INTO THE MINE SHAFT

I remained calm as this new contraption did not make me feel uncomfortable.

If I had been told what would happen next, I'm not sure I would have gone along with it.

When I was in the barn, on my three day "fast" period a mule named "Clyde", an older and experienced mule who had just come up from the mine due to a medical need, told me what to expect.

PREPARING PEARL FOR LOWERING INTO THE SHAFT

"That harness you have been fitted for was designed so that they can attach cables to the harness and lift you up. When they do that, it will appear like you are sitting up like a dog begging for food."

"A dog?!? Now that's funny!!" I thought.

Clyde continued.

"What happens next?" I wondered.

"They'll walk you into the shaft."

"Won't I fall in?"

"No, because the men have placed heavy planks over the opening."

"Oh, that makes me feel better," I thought.

"While you are lifted up, they'll secure your legs to the harness so your legs don't get injured by the side of the mine shaft, as they lower you down into the mine."

"OK, that makes sense to me."

"While you are lifted up, they will remove the plank floor, so you'll be dangling over the open mineshaft."

I really wasn't ready for that, even though I

didn't really understand what it meant. After all, I have always had something solid to stand or lay down on. But what the heck, I'm ready for a new experience.

Clyde then said, "You'll be fine, it just takes a few minutes in complete darkness as they lower you to the level of the mine where you'll be unloaded. There will be planks there and those men, will unhook you and take you to your new underground stable."

Now that didn't seem so bad after all.

And it was just like Clyde explained.

Pete and two other mule skinners carefully attached the top of my harness to a heavy chain and hook that was securely fastened to the center of the mine cage, which had been elevated several feet above its usual position.

Then the hoisting motor began to lift me up so my feet were in the air. And then another line was attached to a different part of the harness and my legs were bound in a leather truss so I could not move. Then they removed the planks and lowered me into the mine.

Thanks to my friend Clyde, because I knew what to expect, it kept me quite docile, as she I felt Pete and the other men involved were taking care of me in this unfamiliar operation.

As I neared the level where I was going to be working, another group of mule skinners grabbed the rope tied to the back of the harness, drew me to one side, and loosened the leg straps so I could stand on my four feet.

It was a strange experience, and when it was over, I couldn't believe I had been in the shaft, slowly being lowered for forty minutes. The time went so fast, and as my eyes got used to the total darkness, I began to feel peaceful.

As I regained my footing, and was led out of the shaft there was a marking that was painted onto the walls near the entrance of the main shaft, and I saw in other places leading to the underground stable.

It read "900 feet".

"I wonder what that means?" I thought.

When I got to the underground stable, it was very different than what I imagined. Almost no light, and no windows. A most strange place indeed.

It was a recess that had been blasted and dug out of the rock.

Once I was taken to my assigned wood stall, and was brushed down and fed, I was left alone. There was another mare next to me, named Marie.

Marie told me about my new home:

"We're in the 'mule drift' which is a stable miners carved out of the rock of the mine. It was long and narrow and had space for twenty-five mules. There was a constant breeze of fresh air that was brought down from the surface. We mules are a valuable asset to the owner of this coal mine, and we are treated with great care to ensure our health and well-being."

And Marie was right, after each shift, I was fed

a diet of hay, oats, and other grains. And fresh water was available at all times.

This is not bad!

UNDERGROUND MULE STABLE

Marie told me our feed was a custom feed blend made just for us so we'd have the necessary nutrition to maintain our strength and energy levels. Each mule at this mine was groomed regularly to keep their coats clean and debris-free.

We had a weekly visit from a local veterinarian, who would check each of us for signs of illness or injury. In case of sickness or injury, the vet would be summoned and promptly he would treat the mule to prevent further complications.

Marie told me that at mines like the Shenandoah #7, the expectation was that once we went inside the mine, we would stay there, pulling the ore cars and helping out until the day we died.

Mules were only taken out of the mine if they were sick, injured, or if the mine was expected to have a prolonged strike.

All of the other mules I met were like me, chosen for work in the mines because we were smart and strong. The miners appreciated us as we moved and carried what the men in the mine could not.

At mine school each of us had been trained to pull heavy cars full of ore in the mine, working all day with few breaks. Marie said that some of the miners had said that we mules worked harder than they did.

No matter what job they gave me that day, I loved the various jobs they gave me and in doing this work, I could tell, I was earning the love and devotion of the miners. I could tell, because these men who spent much of their lives underground developed a deep attraction to each of these mules. And I learned that they depended upon me working alongside them in the dark underground tunnels.

Yes, my new underground home was special, just like me.

And I quickly adapted to it, and it didn't take too long before my miners would call me by name, and give me an occasional treat. I'm guessing it was because of my steadiness and good disposition.

Most days I'd be pulling the ore cars from deep within the mine to the shaft where the ore would be brought out of the mine. Many of the older miners who had worked at different mines before the Shenandoah appreciated these mules recalling working in mines with no mules where they had to push the heavy ore cars themselves, and were particularly fond of me.

PEARL WORKING UNDERGROUND

Some days I pulled mine cars loaded with timbers and other mining supplies deep into the mine where new tunnels were being dug.

This was a good mine. The mule skinners would let me take a rest at different times throughout the day so I didn't get tired. I looked forward to the occasional rest breaks and my heart would leap for joy when Pete, my Mule Boss, would stop by during my rest period. He would always bring Pearl a carrot or something tasty to eat.

"Dahlin', don't let the others know, OK? I don't want them to get jealous."

But at the end of each shift, the mule skinner working with me led me back to my underground stall. I quickly learned that this underground stable had almost everything we had at the mule farm. There was a feed room where feed, hay, and other supplies for the mules was stored, that had storage bins, shelves. Next to it was what Marie called the tack room, where our harnesses, and bonnets were kept. It was next to the wash rack where we were washed and groomed. I looked forward to these occasional sponge-downs to remove the dirt, dust, or grime that would build up on my coat. Then at the very end, was the muck heap where the stable hand would take manure and soiled straw when he cleaned out our stalls.

Every night without fail, Pete would come through the stable and visit each of us mules receiving their daily care. I so looked forward to his nightly visit, and some nights if no one was looking, he might even have a special treat for me and whisper in my ear, "You're special Dahlin'."

Pearl felt blessed to have such an important job and be treated so well.

There's no wonder the miners didn't take long to develop a special appreciation for me, it seems I had a "sixth sense" about me and, on numerous occasions, used my instincts and senses to alert my miners to dangerous situations.

My ears are very sensitive ears and I could hear sounds that humans could not, like cracking, creaking, and shifting rocks or shifting timbers, which could indicate an impending collapse. I quickly picked up the ability to detect the presence of dangerous mine gases, such as methane or carbon monoxide, which could overtake my working miners and expose them to deadly mine explosions.

But one of my best skills was my ability to feel vibrations in the ground. Really!

I can feel the movement of rocks or the earth's

shifting under and around me her, and I've learned to sense even slight changes in the air pressure or mine temperature.

Even as a young mare, I knew I was special, but as time went on, I came to understand that these special skills is why mine mules are much preferred over ponies in the mines; we are instinctually cautious and have been given abilities to sense danger.

So, when I detected subtle changes in my surroundings, I would become restless or agitated signaling to my mule skinner and nearby miners that something is amiss.

My miners seemed to feel a bit safer when I or the other mules were in a working section. When I sense a pocket of mine gas, I'd bray loudly or cough, indicating to the miners the need to quickly evacuate the area.

At the mule farm, I knew the other mules, but that experience is nothing like this kinship between man and beast that I find particularly satisfying to me.

I became totally familiar with working in miles of the dark underground passages. Despite the preventative measures, cave-ins and other emergencies were a part of my life underground. As an experienced navigator, I knew these underground tunnels well, and if something happened in her area, my miners knew I could lead them to the nearest exit.

My miners have become friends, and more like family to me. I look out for them, and they look out for me. Anyone who saw us working underground should be able to see it. We're not just beasts of burden, they looked at me and the other working mules as companions.

Yes, after many years of this work, I had come to love the dead darkness and cherished the miners in my care as they did her. I no longer longed for the daylight above. This was my world.

But one night, after more than twelve years underground, Pete came over to me instead of the mule skinner who normally was returned me to my underground stall. Instead of my usual end-of-shift feeding and sponge bath, Pete whispered, "Dahlin', tonight we'll be going up-stairs."

I stiffened up., as I was filled with fear and anxiety.

"What?" I thought, "Have I done something wrong?"

Unlike my initial trip down into the mineshaft twelve years earlier, the mine had expanded and, with it, a new mineshaft with a much larger cage that could handle more men and heavier material needed in the mine.

Pete led me down the passageway to the larg-er shaft, and together the two awaited the large descending cage. When the cage reached the surface ten minutes later, everything was pitch black, except for the twinkling stars above.

I tilted my head to look up at the heavens. I had not seen such beauty since leaving the mule farm where I was born. "How beautiful!"

Pete led me over to a new barn that had been

built while I was underground that had several stalls. This barn had horizontal boards where the window openings would normally be.

The inside was dimly lit by an overhead electric light bulb. Pete made sure I got my nightly feeding and grooming like she would have underground, but this time it felt different.

"What is happening?" I wondered.

Pete stopped by and gave me a carrot and gently kissed my nose, and then he left.

For each of the next several days, I didn't see Pete, but a stable hand would come to feed and brush me, each time opening the horizontal board a bit wider so that additional daylight could come in.

My eyes, which hadn't seen daylight for many years, hurt a bit at first, but I gradually became accustomed to the light.

I was confused, sad and full of questions:

What about my miners? Who is going to take care of them?

Where is my Pete?

What did I do? Am I being punished?

I just couldn't understand.

As the days passed, I got more and more sad. I missed my miners, and especially my friend Pete.

And I wondered, "Will I ever get to see them again?"

In my many years underground, I had seen many working mules die in the mines and wondered what happened to those that didn't, the ones that became ill and were taken topside.

Were they sold, put down, or perhaps just left to run free?

I wondered "What will happen to me?"

What I could not have known was that times were changing. The mines in Pennsylvania in the 1916's were starting to install electric locomotives. The mine owners had realized that, unlike mules, an electric motor needed no time to rest, stables weren't necessary or veterinarians to keep them in shape. The new electric mine locomotive could haul fourteen cars of coal. The strongest mine mule, at its best, could haul only half that amount.

I awoke on this morning, still confused and sad, but by this time my eyes had now fully adapted to daylight.

The stable hand put my halter on, and I was led out into the small corral outside the barn.

PEARL'S LAST DAY OF WORK IN THE MINE

Then I heard a familiar voice. It was Pete!

"What was he doing here?" I wondered.

Pete came over to her and led Pearl out of the corral and towards a group of men standing in the open.

Immediately my nostrils flared, I stiffened up, very confused.

For I saw the men wiping tears from their eyes.

"Why are all the men present wiping tears from their eyes?" I asked myself.

For the first time in my life, I felt a singe of panic. Pete saw it immediately as my ears pinned back, and began to swish my tail rapidly back and forth.

"Why were her friends crying? What is happening?" I wondered.

As Pete led me closer to the group of men, she saw that it was not only the men she had worked with underground but also some of the people topside who had trained her and tended to her years before. These were men I had worked with and who I felt a connection to.

How could I have known that these men admired me and were crying not in sorrow but tears of joy for me?

As I strode into their midst, the men huddled close around me, gently stroking my neck, back, and shoulders areas and caressing my brown/grey coat.

Later, my lifelong friend Pete would tell her that he had seen the future. As he had watched the new electric locomotive technology arriving at the mine, he understood that the day of mules and mule skinners was ending, and it was time for him to retire. He had asked the mine superintendent if he could take me with him.

With all of this love and attention, I was able to relax and felt an old but familiar feeling wash over me.

"This is peculiar, indeed," I thought. "But I don't mind new experiences."

And with that small and tender family reunion, my Pete gently led me off the mine property to a new future in open and comfortable surroundings on his nearby farm.

CONCRETE CITY

THE FOURTH of July in the summer of 1976 found Eli Smith surrounded by his three children, eight grandchildren, and two great-grandchildren, sitting under the shade of a giant white oak tree at the city park. Two adjoining picnic tables adorned with red and white checkered tablecloths, covered initially with delicious treats, were now empty.

The family had enjoyed a sumptuous holiday feast, and all were full. Eli, looking upon his tribe with great love, asked those gathering, "Now, who wants to hear a story?"

Storytime with Grandpa was always a special occasion, and the parents smiled as the little ones cheered, and young Samuel was the first to raise his hand.

"Tell us about Concrete City, Grandpa!"

Eli leaned back.

"Wow! I did not see that coming!" he thought to himself.

"Okay, kids, here you go!" he said.

"It was 1911, and I was age eight, about your age Samuel. When I first heard the news. I thought, 'This is too good to be true!'

"Our family was being moved from the little hillside shanty to some brand new company housing built at the bottom of the Mountain.

"But it wasn't until I saw the mule and wagon sitting out front of our house in the deeply rutted dirt road that it struck me.

"Mother had loaded the wagon with our few pieces of furniture and had placed my two younger siblings in the back of the wagon with all of the family belongings."

"'Eli, come on!' she shouted.

"As I stood there standing on the tiny front porch, I looked at Mother holding the reins, and all of a sudden, the excitement of the news of a few days was replaced by fear and anxiety.

"I wondered, 'Will I ever see this place again?'

"After all, it's the house where I was born and raised, and all my childhood friends were nearby.

"Not knowing the future was very scary, especially when I realized what I was leaving behind.

"In the days before the move, my father explained that his employer, the DL&W Coal Company, had constructed what the newspapers called a 'model community' for a select group of company employees.

"I listened intently, but I had no idea what a 'model community' meant, but from Dad's explanation, it sounded pretty important.

"Months before, when news of this 'model

community' was first reported to the local paper, it had caused quite a stir. There were to be twenty new housing buildings in this new community called Concrete City.

"From what I was told, it was being built on a former strip mine site and had been leveled out, located near the DL&W's massive Truesdale Colliery, where extracted coal from mining operations was processed and loaded onto railcars.

"When this news was first reported, all of the miners' families wondered, 'Will my family be chosen to live there?' Much speculation and rumor were spreading about the question.

"The Company was not releasing any information, which added anxiety and confusion among the miners.

"My father held the job of section boss/carpenter, a role that the company considered 'essential,' and he told us that he hoped our family would be one of the forty families the Company would choose to relocate.

"But he was wise enough to know that appearing overly eager to Company management could eliminate him from consideration.

"With a massive workforce at that mine, the Company had far more qualified candidates for these new homes than space available.

"Candidates for these homes included Foremen of high-producing veins, Engineers, Blacksmiths, and Electricians who, like Carpenters, were also considered essential.

"So, the company had instituted a selection process that stipulated that these new houses would be rented 'only to English-speaking workers,' eliminating many from consideration.

"But when all was said and done, our family WAS one of those selected, and it WAS moving day.

"So as Mother carefully guided our mule-drawn wagon to the bottom of the mountain, with its contents still intact, you can only imagine the sight that unfolded in front of us.

"I had never seen or imagined such a thing!

"The community where we were now going to be living sat on a massive flat area of almost 40 acres, with the Colliery structures nearby. It had concrete streets and sidewalks. It was amazing!

"I had never seen a street in real life, only pictures of streets and sidewalks in the newspapers and magazines that were passed around from house to house up the hillside.

"But never had I ever seen anything like these houses.

"My heart leapt with excitement when I first spied where we would be living!

"As we came to the bottom of the mountain, I counted twenty houses in the 'Concrete City' development. Each had flat roofs, dark green trimmings, and little red chimneys on the rooftops.

"As our wagon moved into the community, I was struck at the sight! Each building was arranged straight in rows around a central grassy courtyard in the middle of the community.

Mother said that each building had space for two families.

"I saw immediately how Mother's eyes lit up when she first put eyes on the buildings; a broad smile appeared across her thin lips.

"I could almost hear her thinking, 'Oh yes, it was a most pleasant spot of color!'

"As our loaded wagon pulled up on the street before the first row of structures, a neatly dressed DL&W Coal Company official wearing a straw hat greeted us and directed my mother to the building to be our family's new home.

"You can understand I couldn't stop squirming and wanted to jump out of the wagon."

"No, as I told you before we began, your number one job is to look after your two younger brothers and sisters."

"When we arrived at the building that had been assigned to us, I was ready to bolt out of the back of the wagon.

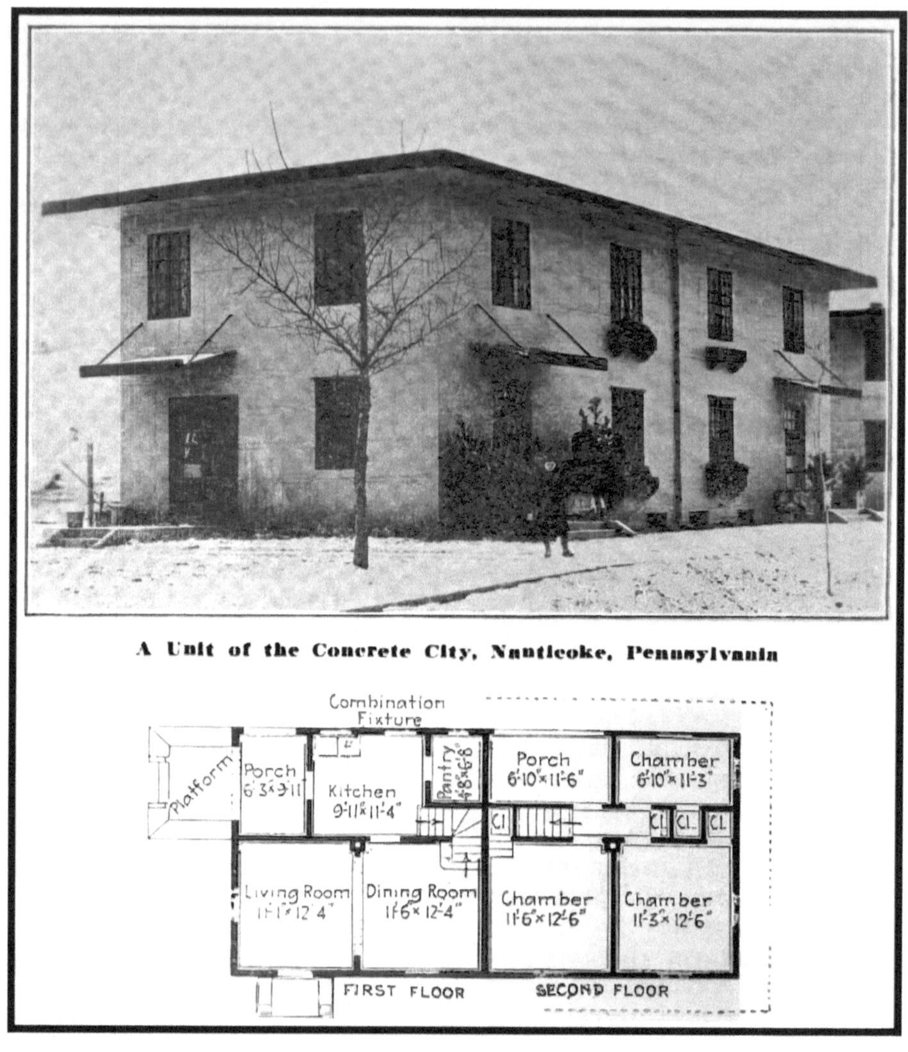

UNIT DESCRIPTION – CONCRETE CITY

"Mother! Can I see our new house?

"I frowned but understood as my siblings had not stopped squirming since being bundled up and put into the wagon.

"It was impossible not to see the pride of the Company official as well, as he took our family inside the unit, we had been assigned in Building 10. He beamed as he showed us through each room."

"These houses have been crafted in one piece from concrete molds. It was an idea of Thomas A. Edison!" he said.

"Now, mind you, I had no idea who that Edison fellow was, but watching Mother nod approvingly, she must have recognized the name and understood its significance as the man continued.

"But when mother stepped into the kitchen equipped with a combination laundry tub-sink and a coal cooking range with a hot water tank, she threw up her hands and squealed joyfully!

"Then the official went from room to room, pointing out each of the unique features of our new residence."

"The floors, walls, ceilings, and stairways

were made using a mold of 'poured' concrete," he continued.

"I had no idea what that meant either. It wasn't very clear, you know!

"Just when I was beginning to think it couldn't get any better, Mother broke down in tears.

"I rushed over to her and asked, 'Mama, what's making you sad?'

"But she shook her head and told me,"

"Eli, those are tears of joy! The man just told me that the way our house was designed, a couple of times a year to clean the house, all we would have to do was move the furniture outside, and the company would thoroughly wash it out with a hose!"

"As she told me about this, her eyes lit up like a sparkler on the fourth of July. Apparently, this was a dream come true – an easy-to-clean house.

"But for me, kids, the feature of our new house was that each building even had a good dry cellar."

"Not only was this a great place to play hide-and-seek, but it meant the summer's produce and a winter's heating and cooking coal supply could be stored safely. I did not like walking out in the cold and snow to fetch a coal bucket from out back.

"As I was thinking about how sturdy our new home was, I imagined living there during the cold, unforgiving Pennsylvania winters.

"All I had ever known was our drafty wooden shanty halfway up the steep hillside. It had been hastily constructed out of slab wood, and the winter winds and snow would come in through the cracks in the boards. My father and mother were always stuffing pieces of cloth and tar paper in the gaps to preserve some heat during the cold months.

"In the background, I could hear the company official going on."

"This concrete structure makes the houses stay cool in summer and warm and dry in winter."

"And there was my mother, shaking her head and saying, 'This sounds too good to be true!'

"Finally, the Company's official tour was over, and Mother escorted the man out. He waved back and left to welcome the next arriving family.

"I'll never forget the tears of joy in Mother's eyes as she stood at the front of the house, gazing upon the little marquises supported by chains overhanging the front steps of all the buildings. Each building had flower boxes on each side, the structures faced a grassy central square where we kids could play, and sturdy wooden benches were provided for the adults. The entire main square area was bounded by newly planted shade trees and concrete sidewalks leading to each structure's front and side doors.

"All day long, as I was helping get my mother and sisters settled, I watched as new neighbors continued to arrive and get settled. Like our family, I hoped our new neighbors would take great pride in these homes.

"Now, as you're listening to me, you might think, 'Why was the Company doing this?'

TRUESDALE COLLIERY AT NANTICOKE PA

"The DL&W Coal Company, which had been very successful up to that time, had decided that this strategy would boost workers' morale and help attract the best supervisory employees that would, in turn, enable the company to keep its experienced miners and above all, improve the company's public image in the press.

"Mind you, it was not a thing taken lightly. In 1911, it was a time when coal companies had a terrible reputation, and the Company was hoping the PR program the company created for the "Garden City of the Anthracite Region" could elevate the DL&W in the eyes of the public as well as the investor community.

"But the company realized that for this 'show-case project' to succeed, appearances had to be kept up to project that image. To do this, the Company offered the residents 'special incentives' to keep Concrete City a unique and beautiful place.

"Behind each building was a plot of ground, which enabled tenants of these properties to plant extensive vegetable gardens in the summer. As appearances were important, Company employees told the residents that each house was to be painted every two years.

"But what I saw Mother get most excited about were the contests.

"One night, after my sisters had been put to bed, I snuck down the stairs and heard Mother describing the contests to Father at the kitchen table."

"You won't believe this! The Company sent a flyer to all residents in this community that they will have a series of contests. Residents with the best-kept and neatest gardens and grounds will be awarded cash prizes!"

"I was too young to understand the significance of this, but Father nodded approvingly. Opportunities to earn cash prizes were unheard of for the women of the coal patches.

"Later on, when I started working in the mine myself, I heard stories from other miners of women living in the other coal camps of the Appalachian region that were taken advantage of when they became indebted to the Company Store. To continue to purchase necessities their families needed, the women would be directed upstairs to meet with the Store Manager to make suitable 'payment arrangements.'

"We knew how vital these contests were to our mother, who had lived a difficult hardscrabble life on the hillside community for so long. We kids got our heads together and devised a plan to help Mother win some of these cash prizes offered by the Company.

"Once we realized how important winning these contests was to Mother, each day after school, we would carefully scout out the entire complex, taking note of the buildings with the best-kept and neatest gardens. We would pay particular attention to blooming florals planted in the first and second-story windows and flower plots around and behind the houses.

"Being as stealthy as possible, when an opportunity presented itself, my sisters and I might even grab a cutting or steal a plant here and there to take back home to Mother.

"Mother, with a knowing eye, would never ask where these 'gifts' had come from.

"Besides these 'scouting parties,' the three of us kids helped Mother work out back in the vegetable garden, which by early summer became filled with all sorts of vegetables we grew. What fun it was to grow our food, and we were delighted when it was big enough to harvest throughout the growing season.

"Up on the hillside, besides scrub grass, there wasn't any place where you could grow much of anything.

"The best part is that we kids knew (even

though we knew this was 'work') that we were also helping support our family in our little way.

"I felt our family had been blessed. We were now living in a style that was so different, one that we never before could have imagined. We felt so blessed!

"Most of the residents of Concrete City, like us, had also planted extensive vegetable gardens and enjoyed fresh produce throughout the growing season. In the spring, using the seed packets the Company provided, the flower boxes of most of the buildings began to overflow with colorful florals.

"And, just as had been promised, the Company repainted each building and trimmed it every two years to make it seem like new.

"But, as time passed, I wondered, 'Why just us?'

"If our forty families got to live in these fancy surroundings, why not build more for the rest of the miners?

"Apparently, this was an experiment that the Company hoped would pay off.

"One evening, as was my custom, I snuck down the stairway and overheard my parents talking in the kitchen. The Company was very happy with the results of the Concrete City arrangement, and it was paying tangible benefits.

"They talked about newspaper stories that reported significant labor turmoil in the coal industry and described many ugly and bitter mines with striking miners and several even getting violent.

"From what my father had told me, all the workers at the Truesdale Colliery were being treated well, not just those living at Concrete City. The idea behind DL&W's 'Concrete City' was to enable the Company to attract a better class of supervisors who ran the day-to-day mining operations, overseeing the daily production operations with fewer issues with the men.

"But my skeptical young mind asked, 'Did it really make a difference?' as I wondered how the other miner's families felt that they had not been as fortunate as ours.

"I got the answer to my question a few weeks later. One afternoon as I returned from school, a note was attached to the brown wicker mail basket that hung by our front door.

"I glanced at it and immediately burst into a scream of excitement. Mom, all of us have been invited to an ice cream social! Now, truth be told, I had no idea what this meant. I had never heard of an 'ice cream social,' but it had to be fun if ice cream was involved!

"Mother sat down at the kitchen table, and a warm smile appeared on the delicate features of her face as she carefully read and reread the invitation to all of the residents of not just Concrete City but all of the DL&W's Truesdale works. The Company invited everyone to hear a major announcement in the main square the following Sunday afternoon.

"Then I saw Mother's brow furrow as another thought crossed her mind.

"What is it, Mom, puzzled by this sudden change of behavior?"

"Eli, these are challenging times in the mining business. I've heard that sometimes when a coal company makes a special announcement, it is to bring bad news. They invite all employees together under the guise of an Ice Cream Social, which could be a way to get everyone to hear it at once.

"Now, we need to keep an open mind, attend this event, and hear what the Company has to say."

"The following Sunday, after our family attended church, we looked at the event unfolding in the community square. I had never seen such a thing. Miners and their families were flooding from the surrounding hillsides into the central square. And the Company, in addition to a huge canvas tent where the ice cream was being served, had set up games for us kids, chairs for adults to sit and chat, and two different places where music was being performed. Nearby was a stage that had been constructed where I assumed this important announcement would be made.

"At the appointed time, the Company Superintendent of the mine and two other company officials stepped onto the stage, and the two groups of musicians stopped playing. The Superintendent welcomed everyone and proudly announced that the Truesdale Colliery had just set a record for the previous year, 1916, for the anthracite coal industry.

"Then he loudly proclaimed, 'I am so proud of all of you. Because of your excellent work, this mining operation produced one million seven hundred thousand tons of coal last year. Please accept our sincere thanks and enjoy the token of our appreciation,' as he motioned for the Ice Cream tent to begin serving.

"The crowd went wild, and the two bands struck up a lively course. Amidst the raucous celebration that followed, I was beaming with pride and looking forward to when I could follow my father into the mines. It was a wonderful thing to work for such a company.

"On my third cup of ice cream, I went up to Father and shouted, 'These are good people to work for!' He heartily agreed. And two years later, as I achieved the 'legal' working age, I worked for them also.

"And for the next several years, the Truesdale mine, where my father and I worked, had a stable, productive, and contented workforce and would remain the largest anthracite-producing mine in the world.

"But storm clouds were starting to appear on the horizon; it began as a notice from the nearby city that Company officials received. When Concrete City was first built, these buildings were touted as an engineering marvel of the day, enabling the Company to construct the buildings quickly and inexpensively.

"But in their haste to construct this model community for miners, the Company had overlooked a trend sweeping the country. By the early 1900s, many cities and towns had implemented plumbing codes that required new buildings to have indoor plumbing, providing residents access to clean water and proper waste disposal systems. Those miners living on the hillside in a two-room wooden shack knew nothing besides a communal water well with a pitcher pump and an outhouse.

"Sadly, that's the way the 20 concrete structures were built. In 1911, there were no codes for indoor plumbing, so it was not a building design consideration. Nobody at the Company had considered whether plumbing could be added later to provide for indoor bathrooms and kitchens. Each residence was connected to a water well with a pitcher pump in the kitchen, and each building cluster had an outhouse building out back.

"The Company's designers and planners for Concrete City had completely failed to consider sewers. In the early twentieth century, local ordinances now required communities to provide water and sewer systems. When the Company received this notice and calculated the cost to add these features, overnight the economics of the Concrete City project went from good to awful.

"The DL&W had silently arranged a sale of the entire Colliery complex to the Glen Alden Company in 1923.

"This sale was not publicized because the new owner of this Colliery was quite different from the DL&W. The Glen Alden Coal Company was one of Pennsylvania's largest coal mining companies in the early 1900s. It was known for its aggressive acquisition of smaller mining companies and its efficient, cost-effective mining operations. It was often criticized for its treatment of workers, who often worked long hours in dangerous and unhealthy conditions.

"The residents of Concrete City became aware of this change, not from an official notice but from word of mouth among the miners. No information was provided to the residents at the time of the sale on how it might affect them.

"Glen Alden's aggressive acquisition process did not realize that the Concrete City part of this new 'investment' was going to end up costing the company hundreds of thousands of dollars (in 1923 dollars) of additional investment in order to install the type of sewer system that required to meet the local township's new building codes.

"So in 1923, a notice was delivered to each resident's brown wicker mail basket that, unlike previous announcements, was no cause to celebrate. Concrete City was no longer under the ownership of the DL&W. The Glen Alden Coal Company was the new owner. It went on to say that the Concrete City property was being shut down. The residents were given two weeks' notice to vacate.

"As you might guess, this announcement sent a shock wave throughout the community.

"Some residents accepted the notice, like my parents, and began to prepare to move elsewhere. Others did not. The ones that didn't evacuate in two weeks were threatened with eviction.

"Eviction processes in 1923 typically involved the property owner initiating legal proceedings against the tenant to obtain a court order for the tenant's eviction. This typically involved serving the tenant with a notice of eviction, followed by a lawsuit or other legal action to obtain a court order. The process could be time-consuming and expensive and often involved multiple hearings and appeals. In some cases, the tenant may have had the right to contest the eviction in court or to request a stay of eviction to allow more time to find alternative housing. Once the court order was obtained, the landlord could proceed with the eviction, typically with the assistance of law enforcement officers if necessary.

"Glen Alden chose a quicker way to evict the tenants who refused to respond to the 'vacate' order.

"Instead of following the usual legal procedures for evictions, the company hired a group of men to dress up in black robes and masks and scare the tenants out of their homes. They hired a group of Philadelphia policemen, who became known as the "Black Robe Brigade" due to the black robes they wore over their uniforms, to carry out these evictions. These men would bang on the doors and windows of the houses, make loud noises, and shout threats and warnings.

"The Company had used these men before. They had become known for their brutal tactics, and companies like Glen Alden had hired them to evict residents and strikebreakers. When they arrived in Concrete City, the evictions were a traumatic event for the Concrete City residents, many of whom had nowhere else to go, and the use of the "Black Robe Brigade" was widely criticized.

"The evictions at Concrete City reflected the power that companies like the Glen Alden Coal Company had over their workers and the communities they built. The use of violent tactics to evict residents was not uncommon at the time, and it was not until many years later that laws were put in place to protect tenants from such treatment.

"The company claimed that vacating Concrete

City was necessary to renovate and modernize the housing complex. However, it became clear that they intended to flatten this complex and redevelop this piece of land.

"My family and I had seen how the benevolent style of the DL&W was being replaced by a more heavy-handed approach used by Glen Alden. Once they received their 'vacate' notice, they began preparing to move out.

"So here we were in 1923, on a Sunday. I spent the day helping my aging Mother and Father load the family's belongings onto a rented truck to relocate to hastily arranged accommodations we had found back up the mountainside not too far from the shanty our family had left 12 years before.

"My Father and I continued to work at the mine for many more years, but the under the new owner, the work experience and conditions were nothing like the years when the DL&W owned the mines. But it was steady work, and we were grateful to have it.

"Each day, as my dad and I traveled to the mine, we passed by the Concrete City site. After Glen Alden Coal Company purchased the Colliery, they had plans to demolish Concrete City's structures and build something new on the site. But as fate would have it, attempts by the company to dynamite the complex failed when these sturdy concrete structures defied even the most aggressive demolition attempts.

CONCRETE CITY AFTER ABANDONMENT

"DL&W had constructed these buildings with

structural concrete, infused with coal cinders and crude oil, and floors, walls, and ceilings reinforced with iron rebar to provide additional strength. After several attempts to demolish the buildings, Glen Alden gave up, leaving the disfigured buildings empty, an 'eyesore' in anyone's opinion.

"So, in the end, the disfigured Concrete City prevailed; the marvel of modern engineering, once hailed as the 'Garden City of the Anthracite Region,' had proven to be a stubborn opponent, seemingly impossible to demolish. It remained a painful reminder to us, who used to live there, that things built with good intentions tend to endure."

Eli paused, looking up and down both sides of the table at the looks of astonishment on the adult's and children's faces.

"There is, of course, an important life lesson here! Does anyone know what that might be?"

Jessica, age 13, raised her hand and spoke up.

"I know, I know," she shrieked.

Eli smiled and invited her to share her insight with the others.

"When you start to think 'This is too good to be true!' be careful! Because it may, in fact, Be too good to be true!"

FOR PEAT'S SAKE

IN JUNE 1891, seventeen-year-old Pete Smith needed a job. His father, a local farmworker, had recently passed away, and the young man needed to quickly find a way to support himself and his mother, who had been in poor health for most of his childhood.

Since there was no one else to care for his mother, Pete, the only child, had left school after eighth grade to be his mother's primary caregiver.

There weren't many employment options in 1891 available in Metamora, Illinois.

The small town of almost one thousand residents was surrounded by rich farmland and farms that supported a handful of in-town family-run small businesses, including the general store, blacksmith, lumberyard, and hotel. Some other residents found stable employment at the local school, church, and post office. Pete felt he had few options besides seasonal low-pay farm work.

To find a steady job, the only other possibility was looking for work out of town, but that didn't seem possible either, as he and his mother were literally dirt poor.

As much as he would have liked to, Pete could see no viable way to obtain decent-paying employment in Peoria, about twenty miles away. The family had no transportation. So, if he got a job, he would have to commute back and forth to Peoria daily.

While a few Metamora residents worked in Peoria, Pete discovered that commuting on the Chicago and Alton Railroad or hiring a horse-drawn carriage or wagon would take several hours of a bumpy and uncomfortable ride, not to mention the significant expense.

Walking that distance was out of the question. So, he was resigned to the reality that neither of the two commute options would work. He needed to stay close to home to care for his ailing mother.

One morning, while stopping by the General Store, he heard that a new business was starting a couple of miles west of Metamora. The company had erected a building that would house a peat processing plant on the banks of the Illinois River.

Mister Campbell, the town Postmaster on Davenport Street, had told the proprietor of the Barber Shop that this new company was looking to hire men with physical strength who knew the local geography and geology. This company intended to extract the best local peat deposits in this area where quality peat was known to be found.

Once the Barber got wind of this, he reached out to Pete, who he knew needed a job.

It was music to young Pete's ears.

"I know this area inside out!" Pete said.

And Pete did. He worked alongside his dad on the many farms to the west of town where they lived. And he was familiar with the extensive peat bogs of the area, which of course, would make the location of this new peat processing plant a natural choice for a peat mining operation.

Central Illinois was considered commercially attractive for several reasons:

Woodford County, in central Illinois, was an area well known for its extensive peat bogs and a history of small-scale peat mining operations. A couple of years before, Pete and his father had worked in a few local peat bogs as miners, which was backbreaking and difficult work, but provided a way to keep food on the table in the seasons when the local farms didn't need additional field workers.

In the late nineteenth century, the standard practice for mining peat involved a combination of digging and cutting techniques. Peat miners would dig trenches or pits in the peat bog and then cut the peat into blocks or chunks using spades or turf knives. Once the peat had been cut out of the ground, it was typically left to dry in the sun and wind for several weeks or months, depending on the time of year. Once the peat was dry, it could be used as a fuel source and was seen as a low-cost alternative to coal.

DIGGING PEAT BY HAND

Pete was among the first men to apply at the

new company's plant. He was confident that this company would need many peat miners like him who had the strength and stamina to cut and haul the heavy blocks of peat dug out of the bogs.

The owner of this new venture was said to be a lady entrepreneur up in Chicago who had carefully studied the market for peat and recognized the potential for commercial-scale peat extraction in Central Illinois.

The company had apparently done its homework on the Metamora area.

Peat, a partially decayed organic matter found in peat bogs, was seen as a potential energy source. Even though at this time coal was a primary fuel used for heating and industrial purposes, peat was considered a viable alternative due to its abundance in the region and the perceived ease of extraction.

It was also becoming valued for its various industrial applications; it could be used as a raw material for manufacturing processes such as tanning, dyeing, and pharmaceutical production, due to its high organic content.

Peat was being discussed in agricultural circles as a key to enhance crop growth and productivity, particularly in regions with nutrient-poor soils like Central Illinois.

Based upon over one year of study and analysis of the area, it was led to the belief that Woodford County was a perfect location for a peat production facility. Its location in central Illinois was already known to have extensive peat bogs and had a history of small-scale peat mining. It had a decent transportation infrastructure, with shipment possible via rail and the Illinois River, making transporting the peat to markets in other parts of Illinois and beyond economical.

The "icing on the cake" for the accountants was that Woodford County had a pro-business climate and offered tax incentives for the company to locate there. All these factors came into play, making it easier for the new company to secure needed financing for this project and obtain the necessary permits to start her peat mining operation.

But the decision to set up this facility in Woodford County was just the first part of this entrepreneur's larger vision.

Years before, in the 1870's, when this lady was growing up in Stockton, California, her interest was sparked by an article discussing peat's potential as a fuel source. At the time, peat was commonly used for heating and cooking in many European countries but was not widely used in America.

This enterprising lady saw how it could be packaged and used in various forms as a clean-burning, renewable resource with other uses as well.

Years of experimenting with different methods of peat extraction led to the development of a successful technique that involved pressing the peat into bricks. These peat bricks became quite popular in the San Francisco Bay Area, where they were used for heating and cooking instead of coal.

These efforts began with a small but successful peat mining operation, with a team of workers extracting and processing peat from the swamps and wetlands of the nearby Delta region, still a primitive area formed by the confluence of the Sacramento and San Joaquin rivers.

However, moves like this venture were opposed by the powerful coal lobby and was publicized as too radical in 1891.

She joined the ranks of women entrepreneurs that banded and, in many cases, pooled their resources to survive and overcome the blatant discrimination and rejection that women of that day encountered in the male-dominated energy industry.

A determined woman who refused to take "no" for an answer required her to persistently navigate the minefield of skepticism of bankers and shippers who refused to take this enterprise seriously. Despite that, each obstacle was overcome, and with time even skeptics gained respect for her innovative techniques and ac-

knowledged this successful peat mining operation.

Beyond getting startup financing, the market economic forces were significant.

Since peat mining was not a widely recognized industry, she needed help finding investors to undertake such a risk, even though she already had a significant peat mining and processing venture in California.

Ultimately, she prevailed, but only after investing much of her personal resources. Still, her ingenuity and perseverance enabled her to establish and build her new peat mining operation in Metamora from the ground up.

Pete had prepared as best he could for this opportunity and showed up in his worn but clean and neatly pressed Sunday suit. Pete sat in the small windowless room outside the office, calm and collected. He knew fieldwork and the local geography, and he and his father had cut and harvested peat for use in their home. So, Pete sat confidently, knowing that any question this interviewer would have about how to locate the best peat, cutting it out of the ground and drying it would be answered with the voice of first-hand experience.

When the door opened, he was most surprised when a little woman, keen, alert, with bright eyes and an expressive face, walked into the interview room. The questions she began to ask Pete were quite different from what he expected.

This woman had a passion for the natural world and a deep knowledge of plants and soil. The two spent the next half hour discussing plants, soil, and the importance of soil health. Because of Pete's years spent with his father, he was very well-versed in these things, and the two had a lively, interactive conversation.

This woman, who introduced herself as Harriet, laid out her plans for this new plant and how she intended to revolutionize how peat was mined, processed, and marketed.

But to make this plan work, she needed a person she could trust who understood agriculture from the ground up, not from a book, but by getting dirt on his hands. That was the person who would be entrusted to oversee this facility. Responsible not only for the mining but also for the production part of the process.

When the interview was over, an offer of employment was extended to Pete. If accepted, he would be the Operations Manager for this new facility. Pete was blown away!

He, of course, knew lots about peat mining and drying it so it could be used for fuel. And, in his years of working around farms, he also had become familiar with different kinds of agricultural machinery. If the truth be told, he was pretty handy at repairing machines that were broken or weren't operating properly.

Harriet was not as concerned about his limited formal education as she was about finding a person for this plant who had local knowledge, perseverance, common sense, integrity, and who was not afraid of the hard work it would take to launch and grow this business.

After regaining his composure, Pete gratefully accepted her generous offer of employment, which provided a regular weekly salary and a bonus he could earn based on accomplishing specific goals.

As Pete left the interview, he was beside himself with disbelief.

"How could this be happening to me?" he wondered.

When he left the house that morning, he had no such thought of being offered this type of work. This job would enable Pete and his mother to live more comfortably.

Starting the following Monday, Pete dove into the work of beginning up the new plant, getting actively involved with learning every aspect of the mining and production activities.

Despite his limited formal education, Pete had a knack for seeing things that could be done with peat. He spent significant time with local farmers investigating how they used peat to grow more healthy and vigorous crops.

He spent his days thinking about how peat could be adapted to these new needs and sharing these ideas with Harriet, who had returned to Chicago but was a frequent visitor to the plant in Metamora. In less than a decade, the company he was managing had developed a range of peat-based products, including:

Peat Fuel: Compressed peat bricks that could be burned as fuel for heating and cooking.

Peat Moss: Sold as a soil amendment in horticulture and agriculture, valued for retaining water and nutrients while allowing for good drainage.

Peat Pulp: Used as a raw material for making paper.

Peat Charcoal: Used in the production of gunpowder.

Peat Wool: The Company experimented with producing peat wool, a material made from compressed peat fibers that could be used as insulation.

And as plant Operations Manager, Pete Smith

confidently fit into his new role. Using his raw intelligence as the Plant Operations Manager, he helped build the venture over the next years.

His "in the field" experience and knowledge of the area enabled Pete to oversee the surveying and selection of productive peat deposits: Coming from a farming family Pete also was keenly aware of the importance of drainage and drying: to lower the water table and facilitate peat harvesting. Knowing first-hand from working the fields with his father Pete knew what a tedious process getting the peat out of the ground, even when using specialized tools such as peat spades or turf irons. He brought new technology to the business to automate cutting through the top layer of vegetation and making it easier and more efficient to extract blocks of peat that could then be turned and stacked to further dry out and harden.

He innovated the processes of transport and stacking, replacing wheelbarrows with carts, and even specialized narrow-gauge rail systems to enable the harvested peat to be stacked in storage yards or drying fields for further curing.

PEAT DIGGING MACHINE, ILLINOIS
Power excavator at work, factory in the distance

PEAT DIGGING MACHINE

He fell in love with peat and it was obvious to everyone with whom he came in contact. His excitement was evident, and if you asked anyone in the area, they'd say it was Pete, the biggest cheerleader of all things, peat. So enthusiastic was he that the townsfolks gave him a beloved nickname "Peat Pete."

This term of endearment caught newcomers a bit off guard. When Pete was walking through town, he was greeted by "Peat Pete, how are you today?" or "There goes, Peat Pete."

Pete's integrity, willingness to do whatever the task required, and raw talent for getting things done, made Pete a "big man in town" and a widely respected local community member.

And the Harriet Strong Peat Company pioneered developing and commercializing peat products in the United States. Its products played an important role in the growth of the peat industry in the early twentieth century.

This confirmed Harriet Strong's belief, evident on the day she first met this local young fellow, that she had indeed picked the right man for the job.

JIM AND HIS RESCUE ANGEL

AS YOUNG James "Jim" Cross, a mining engineer, began his shift the morning of June 16, 1926, he joked to his fellow workers coming onto the property that it would be "just another day."

As it was Friday, he was looking forward to spending time with his girl Clara whom he had been courting for almost six years.

But today would turn out quite differently than he or Clara imagined.

When he reached his workspace, he received word that there had been a fire and an explosion at the Barnes-King Mine, which was near the mine where he was working. The mine located in Silver Bow County, Montana was one of the largest and most productive copper and silver mines in the Butte mining district in the northern Rocky Mountains on the Continental Divide.

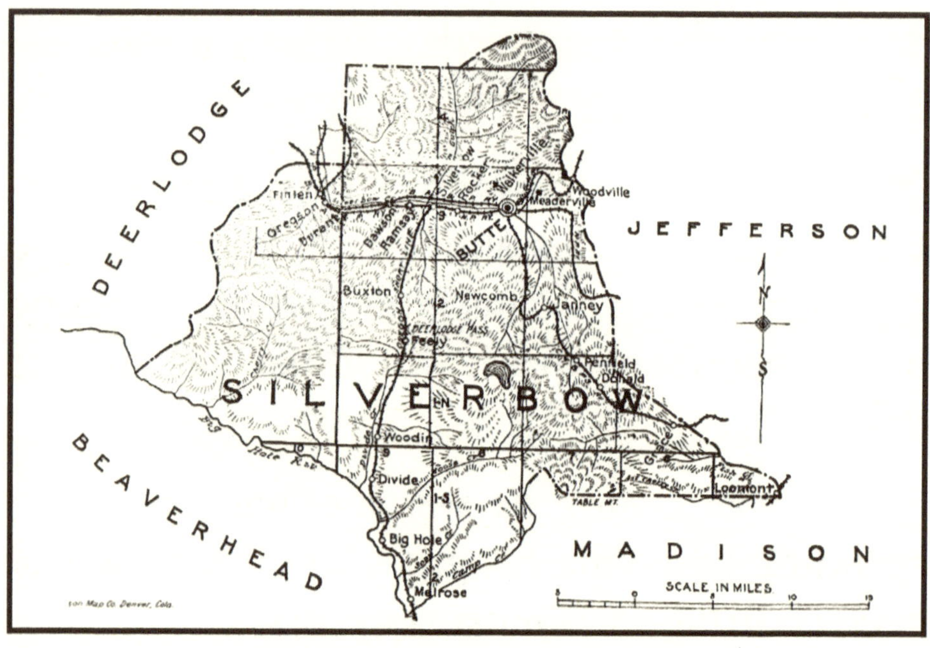

SILVER BOW COUNTY, MONTANA

A fire had broken out in the mine's shaft, trapping twenty-three miners underground. The miners had been working over fifteen hundred feet below the surface at the time of the fire. The mine's ventilation system failed; without it, toxic fumes and smoke quickly filled the mine's tunnels, making it difficult for the miners to escape.

The mine's management had called for assistance from the local fire department and mining rescue teams. Jim was on call to serve in this capacity. He had done so in the past, and when first hearing the news, it took him back to his first experience serving on a mine rescue team nine years before.

There were many similarities between what he heard of today's incident and what he encountered on his first mine rescue experience in 1917. They weren't pleasant recollections.

Mine rescue crews are critical responders to mining disasters and help save the lives of miners trapped underground. When an underground mine incident occurred, they were called upon to provide the following services:

Assess the situation: The mine rescue crew would first need to determine the extent of the disaster and the number of miners trapped underground. They would assess the structural integrity of the mine, as well as determine the levels of oxygen, carbon monoxide, and other gases present in the mine.

Provide emergency medical care: The rescue crew would provide first aid and emergency medical care to stabilize miners before attempting to move them out of the mine.

Secure the area: The rescue crew would need to secure the area around the disaster site to prevent further accidents and ensure the rescue workers' safety. Often, this involved shoring up unstable areas of the mine, controlling the flow of water, or using other measures to ensure that the rescue operation could proceed safely.

Ventilate the mine: Where there has been a fire or explosion, the rescue crew must ventilate the mine to clear out toxic gases and ensure enough oxygen for the trapped miners to breathe.

Enter the mine: Once the rescue crew had assessed the situation, provided emergency medical care, and secured the area, they would enter the mine to locate and rescue the trapped miners. This meant crawling through narrow passages with the limited breathing apparatus of that time, often moving through areas with limited oxygen.

Extract the miners: Once the miners had been located, the rescue crew would work to extract them from the mine. Injured or deceased miners were brought out on stretchers, and those able to walk were led out of the mine on foot. Jim had been on rescues where there was a need to create a new escape route or widen existing passages to allow the miners to be safely removed.

Jim was experienced in all of these areas. He understood from participating in several prior rescues how physically and emotionally demanding this work was. He was effective in this role, requiring skill and quick thinking in high-pressure situations. His efforts had saved countless lives; but sadly, he also had experiences that did not have a happy ending.

So once on station at the Barnes-King Mine, he

jumped right in and, with the other skilled and experienced responders, worked tirelessly for days to reach the trapped miners. When the dust had settled, all twenty-three miners were finally rescued alive. An exhausted Jim sat down, and the imagery of a previous experience flooded his consciousness. When he looked up, he saw his beloved Clara sitting beside him.

Clara saw not only the dirt and grime he was covered in but understood the deeply hidden pain buried deep inside her Jim.

She recalled what Jim had shared about the Speculator Mine disaster in 1917. That mine was considered one of the largest copper mines in the world at the time and was a major source of employment for the people of Butte and the surrounding area. Almost one hundred seventy men were working the mine on another June day in 1917.

The North Butte Mining Company, on June 8, 1917, was installing a sprinkler system at the Speculator Mine to increase safety. The system was nearly complete when one of the last steps required moving a massive electrical cable down into the mine. This cable was twelve hundred feet long and weighed three tons.

Shortly before midnight, as workers slowly lowered the cable, it slipped from its clamps and fell about a thousand feet down the mine shaft. The lead protective sheath of the cable was damaged as it fell from hitting the shaft's rough walls, revealing the oil-soaked cloth insulation underneath. Part of the cable was still snagged on the side of the shaft where it had fallen. About half of the cable that had slipped from the clamps ended up in a tangle at the bottom of the shaft. The rest of the cable remained entangled up the side of the shaft.

The workers performing this task left the cable in the shaft. They reported the incident to the assistant foreman, who then took a shift boss and went down to inspect the damages and locate the cable, carrying a carbide-burning lantern with an open flame.

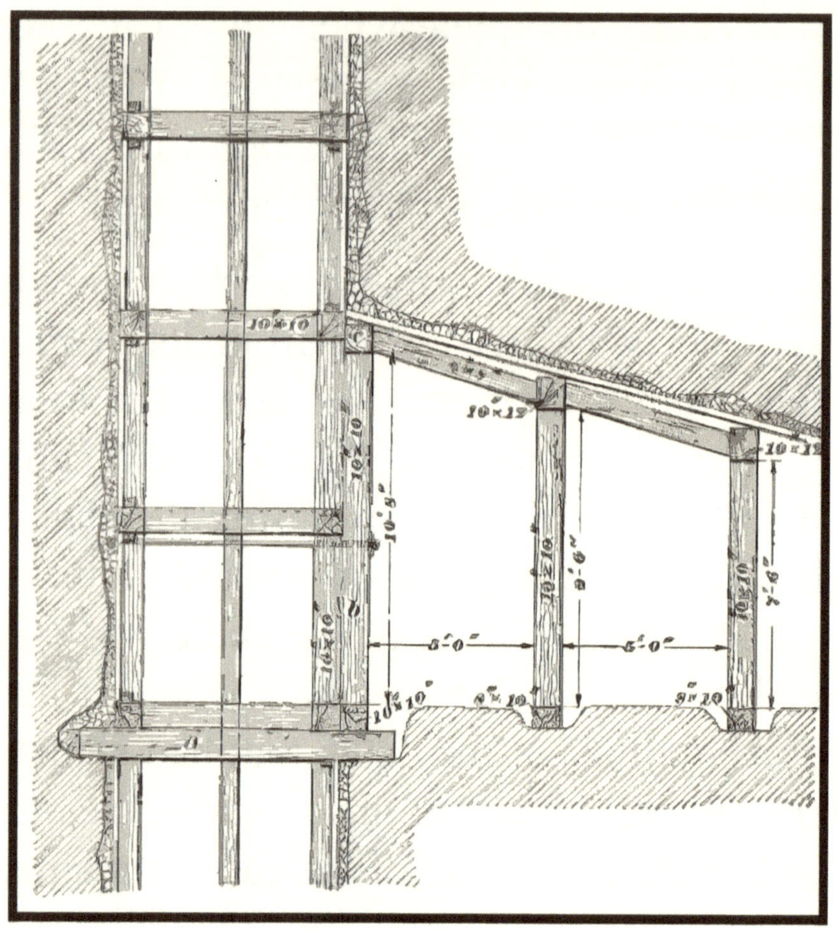

TYPICAL SHAFT AND TIMBERING

As they walked around the tangled cable at the bottom of the shaft, the lantern set a piece of the exposed cloth insulation on fire. In the surprise of the moment, the lantern got kicked over, igniting another section of cloth. There was no way to extinguish the flames. The foreman stayed below while he sent the shift boss above to inform the engineers of the fire.

The part of the cable that was still snagged on the shaft walls at this point was a gigantic candlewick, and the fire had quickly climbed the cable, turning the shaft into a chimney, igniting the timbers in the shaft consuming most of the oxygen in the mine.

The oil-soaked cloth insulation of the damaged cable burned extremely hot and enabled the fire to spread rapidly. Still, it became clear that the fire's acrid smoke and carbon monoxide gas from the blaze became the actual threat as it spread from the shaft igniting upper levels throughout the mine, igniting supporting timbers and fueled by ever-present explosive mine gasses.

It didn't take long before the fire spread beyond the Sunshine Mine into the adjoining Granite Mountain mine. As it spread, it asphyxiated many miners, the raging fire sucking up the oxygen from the air in every workroom, crosscut, manhole, and drift of this maze of underground tunnels.

For the one hundred sixty-eight trapped miners, the rapidly spreading fire fueled by the dry mine timbers made it almost impossible for them to breathe, and the smoke reduced their ability to see.

The men understood that their best chance of survival would be to improvise by finding small, enclosed spaces to protect themselves from the heat and smoke of the mine. Using whatever equipment or materials they found in their sections, they'd try to create a barricade or shelter; lacking that, finding a naturally-occurring niche or alcove in the mine that would protect them.

These seasoned miners knew they must conserve their energy and resources while waiting for the mine rescue people. They knew the rescue crews could take several hours or even days to reach them. But on top of their minds was dealing with the psychological stress of being trapped underground and the possibility that they might not make it to the surface alive.

MINER AWAITING RESCUE

On that day in 1917, the intensity of the fires and smoke in the mine made it impossible for Jim and the other rescue workers to begin rescue efforts. The firefighters were throwing everything they could at this fire but having little success making much progress. It was almost a day later before the fire had been brought under control, enabling the rescue crews to access the mine.

Once inside, it became clear that despite their best efforts, the situation was dire. While some parts of the mine still had fires burning, the rescue workers, with limited protective gear, struggled to navigate through the maze of narrow tunnels and climbed ladders between to try to reach where they felt trapped miners might be. It was exhausting work made even more difficult by constant extreme heat and limited access to food, water, and rest for the rescue workers. First and foremost, the crews' thoughts were getting as many miners to the surface as possible.

Some of the trapped miners were believed to be holed up in recesses where they could escape the fire raging through the mine. But the deeper the rescuers went into the massive mine, there were no signs of any miners. And in many parts, they encountered new fires that drove them out.

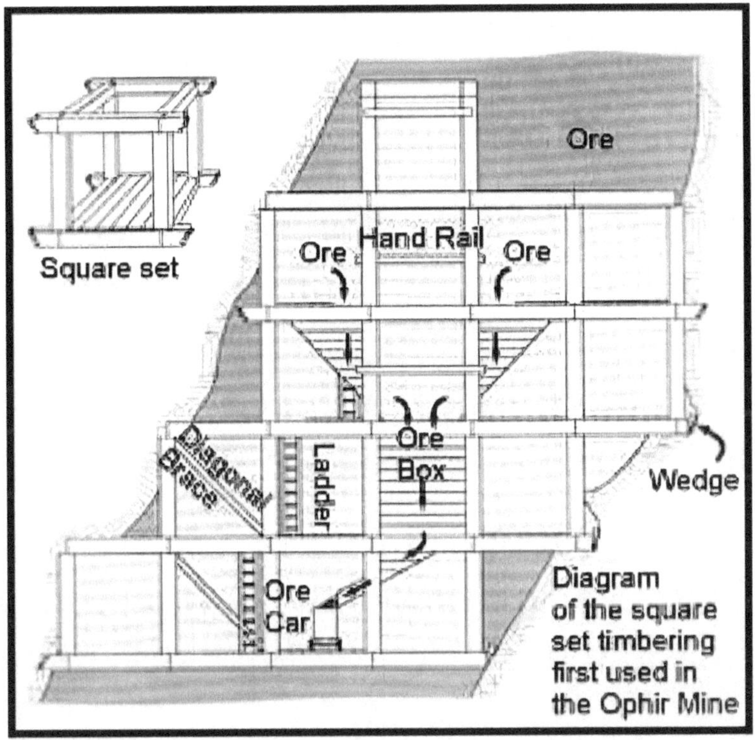

SQUARE SET TIMBERING METHODS USED IN METAL MINES

On June 14th, an order was given to seal the mine to prevent the fire from spreading. The following day, a second explosion occurred in the mine, further complicating rescue efforts. After several frustrating days of trying to contain the fire, which enabled rescue crews to try to locate any survivors that might still be alive, the rescue crews were pulled back. The company decided that the only option left was to flood the mine with water to extinguish the flames. When Jim first described this day to Clara, he broke down in tears.

On June 16, 1917, the flooding of the mine was completed, and rescue efforts officially ended. The final death toll was announced - One hundred sixty-eight miners had died in the Speculator Mine disaster.

Even though it was nine years earlier, this incident's physical and emotional turmoil had taken a long-lasting heavy toll on Jim Cross's spirit.

Today, even though all of the miners at the Barnes-King Mine had been rescued, Jim was numb. While he had been fully engaged underground, his beloved Clara remained topside, outside the mine, providing food for the rescue teams and miners' families that had gathered.

You might wonder, "Who was this kind soul?"

Jim had met Clara six years before.

A young man just beginning his career, Jim worked in mining as most men did, six days a week, ten to twelve hours a day. On Sundays, Jim's only day off, he took advantage of Montana's quiet and scenic beauty outdoors and found a quiet area about four miles away from the mine with a calm stream where he could fish and collect his thoughts.

Compared to his day job in the mines, it gave him a deep sense of peace. He would rent a horse from the local livery to travel to his favorite fishing spot. To reach it, he would go through a village with a small Catholic Church, attending to the spiritual needs of the immigrant settlers of the community.

On one of his Sunday trips, he set his fishing pole outside and went into the service, where he was warmly welcomed. As he was exiting the service, the pastor invited Jim to a church picnic that was being held that afternoon.

Clara, a church member, was a proficient cook and baker and could usually be found at church social events. When Jim arrived, she and other church ladies were setting up for the afternoon picnic.

At his first appearance, Clara's breath was taken away by this striking figure; tall, broad shoulders, with a rugged, masculine appearance. But there was something more she saw.

The couple spoke briefly as Jim passed through the serving station, which gave Clara great joy.

Before he left the tent with his fishing pole, he asked Clara if he might see her again.

His occasional visit to the church became a more regular event. And at Clara's invitation, he and Clara began to enjoy each other's company at Sunday dinner under the watchful eye of her mother.

Over that time, the couple had gotten to know each other. In Jim, she saw the human side of this kind man in conversations and actions that exposed his kindness, honesty, and loyalty.

Raised by her mother, Clara had placed a high value on finding a life partner who was supportive and attentive and who could provide the emotional and social companionship she needed. Jim demonstrated through his words and actions to be a good communicator, had a wry sense of humor, and could listen and empathize when something weighed heavily on her heart.

It was a lengthy courtship, now almost six years, and the couple had lived with the reality that there would be times when weeks or months would go by without seeing each other.

In Butte, the winter season typically lasts from late November to late February. The roads became difficult to navigate due to heavy snow and ice, making them sometimes impassable. And there were times in the springtime and summer when weather conditions such as heavy rain, flooding, or mudslides made it impossible for the couple to see each other.

When Clara received word of the Barnes-King Mine incident, she decided to do something. She packed supplies, hired a horse and wagon, and headed to the mine. She set up a makeshift tent and began cooking meals for the rescue workers and other miners' families waiting for news. Despite the danger and uncertainty, Clara remained steadfast, and her dedication did not go unnoticed.

When rescuers finally reached the trapped miners, Jim emerged weak and ill from the gas exposure.

It took almost a month, but Clara nursed him back to health.

The two were married in a small ceremony at the little Catholic Church in her hometown two months later, and at the service, Jim gave Clara a beautiful silver ring made from ore that had been mined from the Barnes-King Mine.

The couple remained in the area, and Jim continued to work in the mines and, when needed, continued to go out on rescue efforts. And each time he did, Clara also went to provide support.

Clara became known as the "Rescue Angel" for her tireless efforts during the rescue operation. Although losing Jim to health issues at age fifty-five, she continued supporting the mining community for the remainder of her life.

THE POTS AND PANS REBELLION

THE INFANT born in Cork, Ireland, in 1930, named Mary Harris, was destined to become a force to be reckoned with.

Her family migrated to Canada in 1940, and Mary, at age ten, had already experienced the horrors of the Irish potato famine.

Mary was trained to be a dressmaker and teacher in her early years in Canada. She traveled to Memphis, Tennessee, to strike out on her own as soon as she could leave home.

She met and married George Jones, a skilled foundry worker and International Iron Molders Union member.

The couple had four children, but she lost her

husband and all four of their children during the yellow fever epidemic that swept through Memphis in 1867.

Mary relocated to Chicago but lost everything she had in the Great Chicago Fire four years later.

Devastated, Mary looked ahead, and indeed her prospects appeared bleak. She understood what others would see - an aging "over 40", poor, widowed, Irish immigrant woman.

That description painted a picture of one who was as dispossessed as an American could be.

But she was plucky; she had survived plague, famine, and fire. And she wasn't a quitter. She was determined to make a difference in the world and started to transform herself. The first step was to "re-brand herself."

She chose her moniker "Mother Jones" as a way to connect with and inspire the working-class people she had spent her life fighting for. She chose the name "Mother" to emphasize her role as a maternal figure who cared deeply about the welfare of working-class families and their children. The name "Jones" was a common surname at the time, allowing her to blend in with the crowds of workers she often addressed. By adopting a generic name, she could avoid being singled out as a specific individual and instead become a symbol of the larger labor movement.

She shunned the name of Mary, always preferring to be called "Mother." She started wearing antique black dresses in public and exaggerated her age. The new role as "Mother Jones" freed the old Mary Jones from her past.

MOTHER JONES – LABOR ADVOCATE

Most American women of that era led quiet, homebound lives devoted to their families. Women, especially elderly ones, were not supposed to have opinions; if they had them, they were not to voice them publicly – and certainly not in the fiery tones of a street orator.

Jones began to work tirelessly as a Labor organizer, committed to improving workers' conditions, including the horrendous child labor practices of that era.

In 1899 labor working in the coal fields of Pennsylvania was not yet organized.

Many European miners like my grandfather, Michael McDermott, an experienced miner who had emigrated from a coal-producing region of South Wales, ended up working in coal mine communities where working conditions were barely improved from what he had left.

In the U.S. in the late 19th century, coal miners were poorly paid. The dangerous mine conditions and little attention to safety contributed to nearly unbearable conditions at the "Drip Mouth" mine in Arnot, Pennsylvania.

The "Drip Mouth" mine gained its name from the characteristic "dripping" or seeping of water from the mine's entrance or "mouth." This water seepage was a common occurrence in many coal mines due to the presence of underground water sources.

Mother Jones, who had become affiliated with the United Mine Workers of America (UMWA) in the early 1890's, had spent several decades working as a labor organizer and activist. She was painfully aware of the plight of these miners.

Among the abuses suffered by miners was the practice of shortchanging the weight of miners' coal cars. It was prevalent in Pennsylvania coal mines, like the bituminous mine that my grandfather worked in, located in Tioga County in north central Pennsylvania.

This common unethical practice meant the company was deliberately paying miners less for the amount of coal they had mined by manipulating the weighing process.

Coal mining was a vital industry in Pennsylvania during that period, and miners' wages were often tied to the amount of coal they produced. To determine the payment owed to miners, the miners as they loaded the ore cars, would affix a metal tag to the ore car and their loaded coal cars were weighed at the surface before being emptied. However, mine owners and operators would employ various tactics to cheat the miners out of their rightful compensation.

One common method was tampering with the weighing scales or employing inaccurate scales that would consistently show a lower weight than the actual amount of coal. Another approach involved using lightweight cars or adding false bottoms to the coal cars, which effectively reduced the amount of coal being measured.

These dishonest practices were widespread and resulted in significant financial losses for the miners. These miners who worked under difficult and dangerous conditions, suffered greatly and when they discovered they were being shortchanged at the scale, it was the final straw and a general strike was called. The issue at this mine was similar to the plight of other miners and was gaining national attention of labor organizations and activists who were advocating for miners' rights.

TYPICAL MINE SCALE

In the bitterly cold winter of 1899, the strike at the "Drip Mouth" mine in Arnot Pennsylvania had been going on for several months. The desperate and hungry miners at the Blossburg

Coal Company in central Pennsylvania were becoming tired and discouraged. A call went out to Mother who at the time was in Pittsburgh.

"Come over quick and help us! IT'S NOW OR NEVER! The boys are that despondent! They are talking about going back into the mines on Monday."

The stakes of this request were high. The company was actively hiring scabs and had a private company police force that was terrorizing miners and their families. There appeared to be no end in sight. The company's strategy was to starve the miners and further reduce their earnings and benefits once the strike ended.

Upon getting the plea for help, Mother left Pittsburgh, arriving days later by carriage at the frigid mountainous coal camp in Tioga County, Pennsylvania, where the evening's lodging had been arranged under a false name by locals. These accommodations were at the coal company's hotel, the only hotel in town.

In 1899, the Blossburg Coal Company, which

owned the local mines, also owned a significant portion of the town of Arnot, Pennsylvania. The company had established the town as a "company town" to house its employees and their families. It owned most of the buildings and infrastructure in the town, including houses, stores, churches, and schools.

Besides the seven hundred houses they owned in Arnot, they owned several of the town's commercial buildings, including the hotel, the water and sewage systems, the electric power plant, and the railroad station.

The company's control over the town extended beyond physical assets as well. Since the company employed most of Arnot's residents, they had almost total control over their lives and livelihoods. The company dictated wages, working conditions, and even access to basic necessities like housing and healthcare.

Mother first met with the workers and their families at a church outside town on Friday afternoon. She stated her concerns and intentions for coming to Arnot, after which the men slowly shuffled to their feet. But the women defiantly rose, their babies in their arms, and pledged themselves to see that no one went to work on Monday morning.

The "Arnot Hotel" where Mother was staying was a large, three-story building in the town center, near the company offices and the railroad station. It was a relatively comfortable and well-appointed establishment, with amenities like electric lights and indoor plumbing, which were not yet standard features in many parts of the country then.

Unlike many of the company hotels in the Pennsylvania coal region, which had rooms for single men (families were put in small company houses), this hotel was primarily used by company officials, visiting dignitaries, and other guests of the Blossburg Coal Company.

Ironically, despite its relative luxury, the Arnot Hotel was not immune to the labor unrest and social tensions that characterized the coal towns of the era. During the many miners' strikes and ongoing labor disputes of the nineteenth century, the hotel was often a target of workers' anger and frustration. It had seen its fair share of clashes between workers and company officials or law enforcement personnel.

At eleven that night, October the fifth, the hotel housekeeper knocked at Mother Jones' door and told her the company had become aware of her presence and that she had to vacate her room immediately.

A miner collected Jones and took her up the mountain to his cold and drafty shanty, where he gave up his bed so Mother could get a good night's rest.

Early the next morning, there was a heavy banging on the shanty door.

A company official, accompanied by an armed member of the Coal and Iron Police, stood defiantly at the front door as it swung open.

The "Coal and Iron Police" were a private security force hired to maintain order and protect company property. They were empowered by state law to make arrests and carry firearms, and their allegiance was clear – they were the company's representatives, not the community.

"This house belongs to the Company. You all must leave NOW!"

And with that, Mother, the compassionate miner, and his entire family were put out on the street.

The family was given ten minutes to collect their few earthly belongings and put them in a nearby donkey cart. With no place to go, they stood in the muddy street in their night clothes, unprotected from the elements.

After the company official and Pinkerton had gone back down the hill, they were invited to come inside by a neighbor who was not afraid of taking the risk associated with this act of kindness.

Word of this action spread across the hillside miners' shacks like wildfire. Within two hours, all of the mining families had been notified of a clandestine meeting to be held at six o'clock on Saturday morning October the sixth at a secluded barn on the property of a local dairy farmer. This meeting spot was to be held in a community called Landrus, where my grandfather and his family of twelve lived. It had been to Mother by a person who had been at the Friday meeting and was located on a hill a couple of miles outside Arnot. The farmer and his wife were good church-going people and were sympathetic to the plight of the miners at Arnot.

As the couple in the early mountain hours stood outside their barn, there appeared, coming up the hillside from Arnot, a procession of over one hundred and fifty miners and their families heading to the meeting that had been planned at the farm.

At the head of the column was the displaced family pulling the donkey cart with the few sticks of furniture and the family's holy pictures - a disturbing image to all who looked upon it.

How could this heartless company act in such a

terrible fashion? For years after, people recalled the disturbing image of the frightened children with tears in their eyes, walking alongside their father and mother on the way to the barn.

You could feel the rage building in the men, even those who seemed unwilling to confront the Company the previous day. As the meeting began, a group of them stood up on bales of hay in the barn and vowed they would never go back to work in the mines.

The moniker "Mother" Jones was no mere rhetorical device. At the core of her beliefs was the idea that justice for working people depended on strong families, which required decent working conditions.

At that meeting, Mother spoke up. If the men created trouble, they would be arrested and fired. She had a different idea on how to break the resistance by the Company.

Mother Jones had a plan – she had previously mobilized women to act collectively in strikes and organizing campaigns. A clever manipulator of the gender conventions of her time, Jones knew that company guards were less likely to act violently when women were present. Accordingly, she instigated audacious challenges to public authority and private power on picket lines. In the Arnot strike of 1899-1900, she shared her plan to disperse the "Scab" strikebreakers the company had hired: A vote was taken and the miners had agreed that they would not go back to work until the company agreed to their terms.

She spent the next hour organizing an army of the women present and putting together a well-crafted battle plan. The following morning, armed with hammers, pots, and pans, they would descend on the scabs attempting to go into their shift at the mine, making as much noise as possible.

Mother was a fierce field General and had told them what to expect and what to do. No, the company couldn't afford to take on a group of women. To ensure that, Mother had enlisted members of the press to be there the following morning to report what they saw.

WOMAN PROLONGS MINERS' STRIKE

Men Had Resolved to Return to Their Labors.

IN BLOSSBURG COAL MINES

The Female Agitator Stopped Them from Doing This—The Vote to Go Back to Work Was 134 to 24 Against It.

(Special Dispatch.)

Arnot, Pa., Oct. 7.—The strike of the miners appears to be as far from a settlement as at any time during the past three months. A rumor was current that an order had been issued by the Blossburg Coal company for the permanent closing down of the mines. No person could be found to verify the story, however.

About 200 of the Arnot miners held a meeting yesterday, when a vote of the married men with families was taken on the proposition to return to work at the old rate of wages. The vote stood 134 for and twenty-four against the proposition. In the evening a woman labor agitator from Pittsburg arrived here and called a meeting of the miners. Her arguments succeeded in causing the men to remain out, with but little prospect of their returning unless the ten per cent. addition is granted, which the company refused to grant.

LOCAL NEWSPAPER COVERAGE

"Take that tin dishpan and hammer with you, and when the scabs and the mules come up, hammer and howl. Don't be afraid of anyone!"

By Sunday afternoon, the company manager and the captain of the company's "coal and iron police" had gathered. They had heard of a planned "assault" and were standing defiantly at the mouth of the Drip Mouth mine when a "human wave" of angry women descended upon the mouth of the mine from two different directions with mops and brooms and pails of water.

Mother confronted the company manager and began beating on her dishpan and hollering - then all of her army of women joined in with her.

The captain of the guard force reached out and grabbed her shoulder.

"Now you go back home," he said, "I'm afraid you'll upset the mules."

But an angry woman in the mob knocked the man to the ground with a griddle, leaving him cowering in the streambed, and Mother screamed, "To hell with the mules and with you!"

Mules used in mining operations tended to be

well-trained and were accustomed to the noisy and often dangerous environment of an underground mine. However, like any animal, they can be spooked by sudden loud noises and Mother Jones knew that the sharp unusual sound of clanging pots and pans was unfamiliar to them and likely to spook the mules.

From that day on, the women of Arnot kept continual watch of the mines to see that the company did not bring in scabs. Every day women with brooms or mops in one hand and babies in the other arm wrapped in little blankets went to the mines and blocked the entrance to ensure no one went in.

And every night, to disrupt the strikebreakers and prevent them from getting any rest, the striking women of Arnot would take shifts and began banging on pots and pans outside the company housing units. The loud and persistent noise made it nearly impossible for the strikebreakers to sleep or relax. Using noise to disrupt the strikebreakers and scare the mules was successful, as many left Arnot, and the strike was broken.

Day and night, the women of Arnot kept watching the mine operations, the way a hungry vulture looks upon prey, looking for every opportunity to swoop in.

After months of terrible hardships and constant vigilance, the strike at Arnot finally ended.

Inspired by Mother's visit, these heroic women who became committed and took action helped change labor and safety practices in the mining industry.

But effecting a meaningful change in any industry happens slowly, and the mining industry of that time was one of the most reticent.

This same mining operation in Arnot brought tragedy to my family. Several years later, my grandfather lost his life in a mine accident in 1913 that left his twelve children without a father.

Hearing of this calamity at Arnot, Mother sent

a wire to the miners, restating her commitment to continuing the fight on behalf of the miners.

It read: "Mourn the dead, fight like hell for the living."

In the years that followed, labor relations at the company continued to be tense. More strikes led to more violence and unrest, with several people injured in clashes between striking miners and company guards. Despite the ongoing labor disputes and violence, the Blossburg Coal Company continued to operate for many years.

Mother Jones played a significant role in encouraging miners to organize in the late 19th century at many mining operations. Still, these efforts were often met with resistance from coal companies and frequently involved violent conflicts. Decades later, legislation was passed to provide miners with improved wages and better working conditions.

But all these improvements being fought for came at a steep price, paid by past generations of miners and their families. While the mining companies paid lip service to concessions they said they would make, they continued to lobby against mining reforms and post record profits. But the ongoing dangerous working conditions had left many coal miners with injuries, illnesses, and premature death. These families were left to cope with the loss of their primary breadwinner and often faced significant financial hardship.

And Mother Jones continued to be active in the labor movement well into her eighties. In her final years, before she passed at ninety-three, she continued to speak out on issues such as child labor, workers' rights, and social justice. After her death, Jones was buried in the Union Miners Cemetery in Mount Olive, Illinois, alongside many of the miners she had fought to organize and support throughout her life. Her legacy continues to inspire labor activists and social justice advocates to this day.

THE BUSINESS CAR

HAVE YOU ever had a REALLY bad job?

Or if not, did you ever see a job that someone else had that you knew you NEVER wanted, no matter what it paid?

In 1910 Leroy Spitten had such a job. He worked at a large portal mine in Montana, a metal mine that went deep into the side of the Rocky Mountains. Unlike the deep underground mines where the company had to dig straight down, a portal mine is designed to access veins of rich ore found in the interior of these mountains. It had begun years before by driving a sloping main tunnel and then off this main tunnel, other tunnels were dug that branched off, following the veins of ore.

It took a special breed of man to endure the conditions under which they worked. A ten to twelve-hour shift was the norm, six days a week, often breathing in rancid air due to poor ventilation. Ventilation systems of the day were very basic, consisting of a large fan at the mouth of the mine that circulated air into the mine shaft and tunnels. This was seldom enough to avoid the heat and harmful gases, dust, and fumes common in mines. The men worked all shifts with little or no lighting except for the few lamps in the main tunnels and small lights or candles on their miner's hats. Hour after hour, they drilled, blasted, clawed, and loaded ore onto nearby mine cars, ever exposed to this equipment, injuring or killing them. What ore the miners dug, they might not be paid properly for as the person running the scale might recorded less than the actual weight, which meant the miner got cheated.

To eke out a bare existence, these fearless souls worked in unstable rock formations, where the risk of cave-ins was high, and each shift they bet against the chance of being buried alive. Deep beneath the earth, these mines, hot and humid, created uncomfortable and exhausting working conditions that could suck the life out of a man.

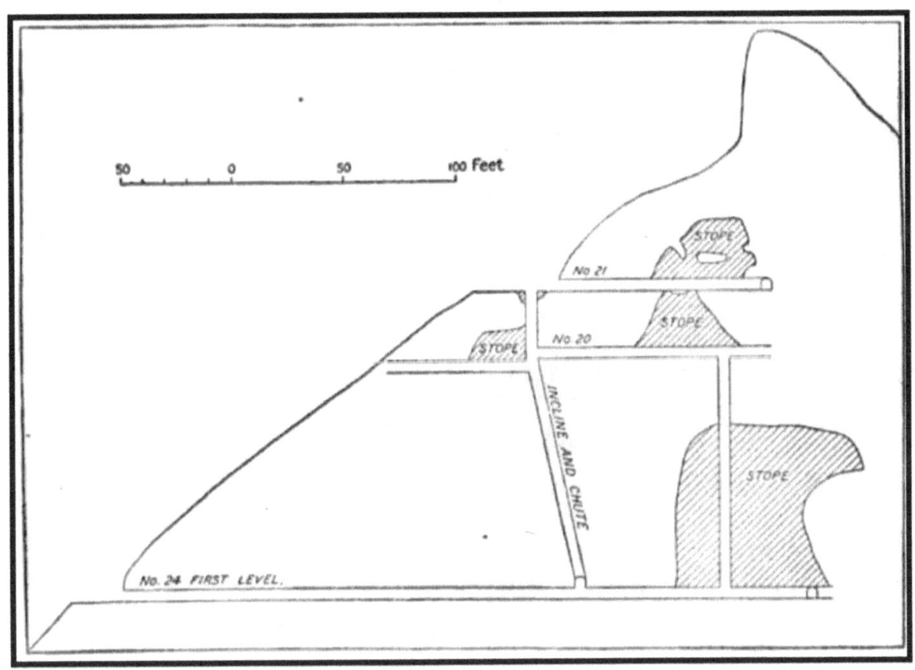

CROSS SECTION OF A DRIFT MINE

Most mine operators were more concerned with profits than safety. Management often ignored dangerous situations, and if there was any safety equipment at all, it was scarce and often inoperable. Any hope a miner had of getting back topside at the end of their shift was largely determined by their own judgment and experience to stay safe.

All in all, you might say, being a miner could be seen as a pretty crappy job to have.

Leroy's job was crapper than most.

He had a specially constructed mine car that he pushed from section to section of the mine. Like the ore cars, it was loaded by the miners, and when it was full, it was taken topside, but there was no weighing of its contents, and not a penny was paid to any of the miners who had helped load it.

For you see, the "special car" that Leroy was responsible for was the "Toilet Car."

To better understand Leroy's job, a bit of background may be helpful:

It's a biological fact - everyone has to relieve themselves at some point. The underground miners who spent their ten to twelve-hour shift underground were no exception. You didn't have the option of going to the surface for restroom breaks. So they went whenever and wherever there was an open spot to do their business.

Put yourself in the miners' place.

How would you feel about your co-workers going to the bathroom a few feet away and then having to work in the smell, or worse, knowing that the water you're standing in includes the runoff from your co-worker's toilet breaks?

Until the early twentieth century, that's the way it was until a major mining company in Montana designed a mine car initially called on blueprints "a toilet car." It was a name that appeared in a few trade publications, but despite its public health benefits not presented that way to the general public.

For, in 1910, people in polite society did not discuss toilet matters openly. Such things were considered taboo.

Discussions about bodily functions and personal hygiene were considered impolite and inappropriate for public discussion. Instead, people used euphemisms and indirect language to refer to toilet matters. For example, "restroom" or "bathroom" was not commonly used in 1910. Instead, people would refer to the "necessary room" or the "water closet." The term "toilet" was used, but it was considered a somewhat vulgar term, and people would often use euphemisms like "powder room" or "ladies' room" instead.

Even in written materials, such as newspapers and books, descriptions of toilet matters were often vague and indirect. Authors would use euphemisms, metaphors, or another indirect language to refer to bodily functions or personal hygiene.

So, the "toilet car" was thoughtfully given a pseudonym, "the Business Car," a term much more acceptable to the general public in the day and one the underground miners understood, laughed about and greatly appreciated.

The "Business Car" body looked like a rectangular steel tank on a set of mine car wheels. It was constructed of one-inch-thick steel plate and had two "outhouse" style openings on top.

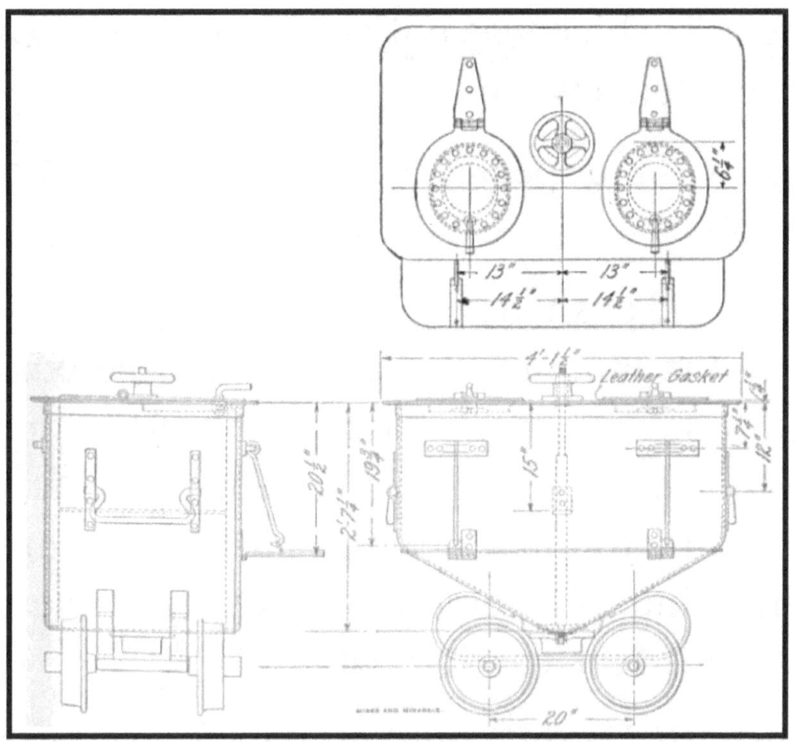

"BUSINESS CAR" DESIGN

Each oval opening had a padded leather seat, and when the opening was not in use, it was covered by a hinged steel lid with a handle to secure it while in transit, enabling the car to be moved from section to section of the mine without any of the contents splashing out.

But the most important feature of the car was between the two seats; an iron hand wheel that operated a discharge valve located at the bottom of the car, which was only used to empty the car of its contents when full.

That was the special car that was Leroy's full-time job.

He would push the Business Car from one section of the mine to the next, secure the wheels using a set of wheel chocks, and wait for the men to use the car. As time went on, when the car became full, he carefully pushed the car out of the mine to a remote site, dumped the car, and cleaned the car. Repeat.

Dutifully, Leroy would do his job. And it was very appreciated by the miners, who anxiously awaited his arrival in their section of the mine. Unlike the roving underground mine bosses, he was one of the people the miners looked forward to seeing throughout the day. Leroy knew his job was necessary and took the job very seriously.

Upon arriving in each section, Leroy would first try to position the car in as flat a spot as he could find and then place the two steel wheel chocks under the car's wheels. A steel chain attached these chocks to the car and each other. When business had been taken care of, and the car was ready to be moved, Leroy would pull the chocks out by giving the chain one stiff tug, secure the chocks to the side of the car, and then push the car to the next section of the mine.

There were two unwritten "Cardinal" rules that the miners knew were not to be violated – EVER!

1) NEVER – EVER touch the hand wheel between the two seats, and

2) UNDER NO CIRCUMSTANCES, mess with the chain attached to the wheel chocks.

And this is how it went, day after day, Leroy appearing with his car, working from section to section of the mine. When it reached capacity, he would push the car outside past the big ventilating fans that were located at the mouth of the mine to a distant location outside. Once there, Leroy carefully positioned the car over a specially constructed waste dump and, turning the iron hand wheel, emptied the car's noxious contents. Next came hosing down the inside of the car, and closing the dump valve, followed by adding some water and a little chloride of lime.

"BUSINESS CAR" PHOTO

Now the car was ready to resume service. Leroy would push the car back into the bowels of the mine.

Mining was a dangerous and serious business, and miners had a way of dealing with new men that proved challenging to work with. In this particular mine was a new man named Kennedy, who had a nasty and disagreeable side. Even though it was his first shift, the miners in his section had already taken a dislike to him.

When Leroy came along that morning, the men explained to Kennedy that this was the "Business Car" without saying anything more. At the first opportunity, pushing another miner aside, Kennedy jumped atop the "mobile throne" and began attending to his biological necessities.

Unbeknownst to Kennedy, the fellow he had pushed aside had slipped behind the car and pulled out the wheel chocks.

He didn't realize it at first, but Kennedy, in a most unprepared position, started to feel the car begin to roll down the tracks.

Leroy had been talking to one of the other

miners and was not paying attention, and when he heard Kennedy scream, he looked up and realized what was happening.

He began to run down the tracks after the fleeing toilet car, which was quickly picking up speed. The men had not told Kennedy about the unspoken "rules" of the car.

As the car gained speed and began to rock back and forth with the sloshing contents inside, Kennedy looked for a way to bring this thing to a halt. Seeing the hand wheel next to where he was sitting, he assumed it was some braking mechanism.

He turned the hand wheel next to his seat as fast as he could, but with each turn, the car only seemed to pick up more speed, and as the dump valve had been opened, it slowly began to release the car's contents onto the tracks below.

Realizing his actions weren't working, Kennedy pulled up his breeches and jumped off the car to safety at the first spot he could find.

And Leroy, who had tried running after his

car, began slipping and sliding on the deposits left between the rails, watched with a horrified look as his car disappeared into the dark recesses of the tunnel ahead.

Now with the lids of the car wide open and picking up more and more speed, the car careened wildly from section to section, with its noxious contents sloshing from side to side. As it reached the mouth of the shaft, the careening car left the rails, crashing head-on into the structure that housed the machinery that operated the massive Guibal mine ventilation fan.

The mine superintendent was not pleased, as the damage to the fan house was significant, without ventilation, the mine could not operate until the fan was repaired, essentially shutting down the mine for two shifts, and Leroy, who was solely responsible for his car, faced strict disciplinary measures.

The mine superintendent knew they couldn't fire him because, frankly, who else would want to do that job?

FAN HOUSE

So today, it's my pleasure to share with you the origin of two commonly used idiomatic expressions that owe their existence to this bizarre incident:

"Don't pull my chain." and "When the shit hit the fan!"

The End

GLOSSARY

Adit: A horizontal tunnel that provides access to the underground mine from the surface, typically driven into the side of a hill or mountain.

Air drill: A drilling machine powered by compressed air.

Air shaft: A vertical shaft used to bring fresh air into the mine.

Assay Office: A building where samples of ore are analyzed to determine their composition and value, often equipped with laboratory equipment and chemical reagents.

Assayer: A professional who analyzes and determines the quantity and quality of metals in ores.

Backfill: The process of filling excavated areas or voids in the mine with waste material, such as rock fragments or tailings, to provide support and prevent collapse.

Bagger: A child who bagged coal for sale or transportation.

Bank Boss: The supervisor responsible for overseeing the coal sorting and processing operations at the surface.

Banker: A young worker who managed financial transactions related to mining operations.

Banksman: A person who supervised the movement of mine carts and wagons at the surface.

Black Cleaner: Workers who cleaned and sorted coal after it was extracted, removing excess dust and impurities.

Black damp: A mixture of gases, primarily

carbon dioxide that can be deadly in high concentrations.

Black Hat: A slang term for an inexperienced miner, often used for those new to the industry.

Black Powder Man: A person who handles and stores black powder, an explosive used in mining.

Blacksmith Apprentice: A young worker learning the trade of a blacksmith, responsible for forging and repairing mining tools.

Blacksmith Shop: A workshop where blacksmiths work to forge and repair mining tools, such as picks, shovels, and drilling equipment.

Blacksmith: A skilled worker who forges and repairs tools and equipment used in the mine.

Blacksmith: Skilled workers who maintained and repaired mining tools and equipment, often specializing in forging and shaping metal.

Blaster: An individual who handles and detonates explosives for blasting purposes.

Blasting cap: A small explosive device used to initiate larger explosions.

Boarding House: A building or lodging facility where miners who are not local residents can live and sleep during their shifts.

Boiler House: A building that houses the steam boilers used to generate power for the mine's machinery and equipment.

Bore Runner: A young worker who operated drilling machinery to create holes for explosives.

Borer: A child responsible for operating a drilling machine to create holes for blasting.

Borer's Assistant: A child who assisted a borer in drilling holes for blasting.

Boss Boy: Young boys who assisted mine supervisors or foremen by performing various tasks, such as carrying messages or tools.

Bottomer: A young worker responsible for operating the winding gear at the bottom of the mine shaft.

Brattice Builder: Workers responsible for constructing temporary partitions or walls (brattices) to control ventilation in the mine.

Breaker Boy: Young boys employed to pick out impurities, in the Breaker Building such as rocks and slate.

Bucker: Workers who manually loaded coal into wagons or rail cars at the surface.

Bucketman: A worker who operates a bucket or skip used for transporting ore or waste rock.

Butty: A term used to describe a skilled miner who worked alongside and supervised a team of other miners.

Cage Tender: Individuals responsible for operating the elevator (cage) that transported miners and equipment between the surface and the underground levels.

Cage: A device used to transport miners and materials up and down the mine shaft.

Caller: A person who announced the work shifts and organized the miners' schedule.

Cap rock: The layer of rock that sits on top of a mineral deposit.

Carpenter Shop: A workshop where carpenters construct and repair wooden structures and equipment used in mining operations, such as timber supports.

Carpenter: A person who constructs and maintains wooden structures in the mine.

Checker: A child employed to count and record the number of coal-filled carts leaving the mine.

Chipper: A child who chipped away rocks and debris from the mine walls or roof.

Chute: A sloping channel or passage used to move ore or waste material within the mine.

Coal Bin: A container or storage structure used

to hold and store coal, which is commonly used as a fuel source for steam engines and boilers.

Coal Breaker: Workers stationed at the surface who sorted and crushed coal into different sizes before it was transported for further processing.

Coal dust: Fine particles of coal that can be explosive when suspended in the air.

Coal face: The exposed vertical surface of a coal seam where mining takes place.

Coal Getter: A general term referring to any worker involved in extracting coal from the mine.

Coal Hauler: Workers responsible for manually loading and hauling coal from the mine face to the surface using carts or sleds.

Coal miner: A person who works underground to extract coal.

Coal operator: The owner or manager of a coal mine.

Coal pick: A hand tool with a pointed end used for breaking up coal.

Coal Screener: Employees who operated machinery to separate coal into different sizes based on its intended use.

Coal seam: A layer of coal that is typically horizontal or gently inclined.

Coal Trimmer: Workers responsible for manually cleaning and removing impurities from coal before it was loaded onto ships for transportation.

Coal washer: A facility used to clean and separate coal from impurities.

Coal Washers: Individuals who operated machinery to separate impurities from raw coal, improving its quality before it was transported for sale.

Company Store: A building or shop owned by the mining company, where miners or their families can purchase goods and supplies, often using company-issued tokens or scrip.

Compressor House: A building housing the air compressors that provide compressed air to power pneumatic tools and machinery in the mine.

Concentrator: A building or facility where the crushed ore is further processed to separate valuable minerals from the gangue (worthless material).

Cornish pump: A type of pump used to remove water from mines.

Crib: A framework of timber or steel used for roof support in underground excavations, typically constructed in a box-like configuration.

Crib House: A structure or building used for storing timber or wooden cribbing used as supports or reinforcements in underground mine workings.

Crib: A framework of timbers used to support the roof or walls.

Cribbing: The process of building supporting structures using timber or other materials.

Crosscut: A horizontal tunnel that intersects the main drift or other tunnels, enabling miners to reach different sections of the mine or extract ore from multiple directions.

Crosscut: A horizontal tunnel that intersects the main vertical shaft.

Crossheading: A short tunnel driven from the main drift or another tunnel to access a specific orebody or working area.

Crusher Mechanic: A skilled worker who repairs and maintains crushing machines.

Crusher Operator: A worker who operates a crushing machine to reduce the size of ore or rock.

Crushing Plant: A building or structure where the mined ore is crushed into smaller fragments or particles, usually using machinery like crushers and mills.

Cutter: A machine used to undercut the coal face for extraction.

Cyanide Plant: A building or facility where gold or silver ores are treated with a cyanide solution to dissolve the precious metals, enabling their extraction.

Decline: A sloping tunnel or ramp used for transportation and access between different levels of the mine, descending from the surface into the underground workings.

Drawer: A young worker responsible for pulling coal-filled carts from the face of the mine to the surface.

Dredger: A child employed to clear debris and sediment from underground waterways.

Drift: A horizontal tunnel or passageway that follows the mineral deposit, providing access to ore bodies or connecting different parts of the mine.

Drift Miner: A miner who excavates horizontal tunnels to access ore bodies.

Drift Runner: A child who operated a cart or wagon in an inclined mine tunnel or drift.

Drift: A horizontal tunnel or passage driven into the mine for exploration or access to working areas.

Driftsman: Skilled workers responsible for excavating horizontal tunnels (drifts) in the mine, often used for ventilation or transportation.

Driller: A skilled worker who operates drilling machinery to create blast holes for explosives.

Dry gangue: The non-valuable material that is separated from ore during the milling process.

Drywasher: A device used to separate gold from dry placer deposits using air and vibration.

Dumpman: A young worker who cleared and maintained areas where coal and waste materials were dumped.

Dust mask: A protective mask worn by miners to filter out coal dust.

Engineer: A professional responsible for designing and managing the technical aspects of the mining operation.

Engineer's Office: A building or space where mining engineers and surveyors carry out planning, design, and analysis of mining operations.

Face Boss: A miner who supervises the work at the "face" or mining area.

Face Worker: Miners who worked directly at the coal face, extracting coal using hand tools.

Face: The exposed area of the mine where mining operations are carried out.

Fan House: A building equipped with large fans to circulate fresh air into the mine and exhaust stale or hazardous air, maintaining ventilation for miners.

Fan Tender: Individuals who operated the

mine's ventilation fans, ensuring a constant supply of fresh air to the underground areas.

Fan: A machine used to circulate air in the mine ventilation system.

Fire assay: A method used to determine the quantity of precious metals in ore samples.

Fire boss: A mine official responsible for inspecting for fire and explosion hazards.

Fire damp: Methane gas, which can cause explosions in coal mines.

Floor: The bottom layer of rock or strata below the coal seam.

Foot Runner: Young boys who ran errands, such as delivering messages or supplies, between different areas of the mine.

Gallery: A large, often horizontal, tunnel or passageway in the mine, typically used for transportation or as a main access route.

Gallery Stoop: A small excavation or platform

within a gallery where miners can stand or work temporarily.

Gob: A term used to describe abandoned or waste-filled areas in the mine, often resulting from previous mining activities.

Gold pan: A shallow metal pan used to separate gold from sediment by washing and swirling.

Gold rush: A period of feverish migration of workers to areas where gold has been discovered.

Greaser: A young worker responsible for lubricating machinery and equipment in the mine.

Guard House: A small building or structure where security personnel are stationed to control access to the mine and ensure safety and order.

Hand steel: A handheld chisel or pick used for breaking rock.

Harness Maker: the person who crafted the harnesses and bonnets for mine mules.

Haulage Boy: A young worker who transported coal or other materials within the mine using horses, mules, or wagons.

Haulage Engineer: An individual who plans and manages the transportation of ore and waste materials within the mine.

Haulage: The transportation of coal or materials within a mine.

Headframe: Also known as a gallows frame or pit frame, it is a structure atop a mine shaft that supports the hoisting mechanism and guides the lifting of men and materials in and out of the mine.

Hewer: An experienced miner who used hand tools to extract coal from the face of the mine.

Hoist House: A building that houses the machinery responsible for lifting or hoisting miners, equipment, and materials in and out of the mine shaft.

Hoist Operator: The person in charge of operating the machinery that lifts and lowers miners and materials in the mine shaft.

Hoist: A machine used to raise and lower the cage or other equipment in a mine shaft.

Hooker-on: A child who attached loaded coal carts to hauling ropes or chains.

Hospital: A building or medical facility located on or near the mining site, providing medical care and treatment for injured or sick miners.

Incline: An inclined tunnel or ramp used for transporting miners, materials, or ore between different levels of the mine, typically at a moderate gradient.

Jackleg drill: A handheld drilling machine operated by a pneumatic leg.

Jig: A device used to separate minerals based on their density.

Jigman: A worker who operates a jig machine to separate minerals based on density.

Laborer: General term for workers involved in various manual tasks around the mine, such as moving materials or clearing debris.

Lamp Boy: A child who carried a lamp to provide light for miners working underground.

Lamp House: A building dedicated to storing and maintaining safety lamps, which provided illumination for miners underground.

Lamp room: A designated area in the mine where miners store and maintain their lamps.

Lampman: Workers responsible for distributing and maintaining safety lamps used by miners to detect the presence of dangerous gases.

Loader: A child who loaded coal onto carts or wagons for transportation.

Lode Miner: A miner who extracts valuable minerals from a mineral deposit or vein.

Lode: A mineral deposit that is embedded within a rock formation.

Machine Operator: A worker who operates mining machinery, such as drills, pumps, or hoists.

Manway: A small passageway or ladderway used for vertical access between different levels or compartments within the mine.

Marker: A young worker who marked the locations of coal seams or other mining features.

Mason: A child worker who built and repaired mine structures using stones, bricks, and mortar.

Masonry Shop: A workshop where stonemasons work on the construction and repair of stone structures, such as walls and foundations.

Mine car: A wheeled vehicle used to transport coal or other materials within a mine.

Mine Engineer: Professionals responsible for

designing the layout of the mine, planning the extraction process, and ensuring efficient coal production.

Mine Foreman: The supervisor responsible for a specific section or area within the mine, ensuring that work is conducted safely and efficiently.

Mine Inspector: A government-appointed official who inspects mines to ensure compliance with safety regulations and other legal requirements.

Mine Owner: The individual or company that owned and operated the coal mine.

Mine Superintendent: The highest-ranking official in charge of overseeing the entire mining operation.

Mine Surveyor: Professionals who measured and mapped the mine's underground workings, ensuring accurate records of its layout.

Mine: An underground excavation where coal or other minerals are extracted.

Miner: The individuals who extract coal or other minerals from the mine face using hand tools such as picks and shovels.

Miner's Cook: A worker responsible for preparing meals for the miners in the mining camp.

Miner's Helper: A laborer who assists miners with various tasks in the underground operations.

Miners' lamp: A personal lamp carried by miners for illumination.

Miner's Lampman: A worker responsible for inspecting, refilling, and maintaining the miners' safety lamps.

Mining claim: A legal right granted to an individual or company to explore and extract minerals from a specific area.

Mucker: A machine used to load ore or waste material into mine cars.

Mule Boss: A person who oversaw the management and care of the mules used for transporting coal underground.

Mule Drift: An underground stable where mules were housed and cared for during mining operations.

Mule Driver: A child worker responsible for driving and handling mules used to transport coal in underground mines.

Mule Skinner: A worker who drives and cares for the mules used to transport materials inside the mine.

Mule: A work animal used to pull mine cars or transport materials underground.

Muller: A small tunnel or drift connecting two parallel tunnels, often used for ventilation or emergency escape routes.

Nipper: Workers who assisted miners by performing tasks such as moving tools, equipment, and supplies underground.

Nugget: A small piece of precious metal, typically gold, found in its natural form.

Office Building: A structure where administrative tasks, record-keeping, and management of the mine's operations are conducted.

Ore Bin Loading Station: A designated area or building where the mined ore is loaded onto rail cars or other transport vehicles for shipment.

Ore Bin: A container or storage structure used to hold and store the mined ore before it is transported to the processing facilities.

Ore cart: A small wagon or cart used to transport ore or waste material within the mine.

Ore Dresser: A specialist who prepares ore for smelting by removing impurities and concentrating valuable minerals.

Ore Dryer: A building or structure used to remove moisture from the mined ore before further processing, reducing the weight and improving its handling.

Ore Sorter: A worker who manually separates valuable ore from waste rock.

Ore Sorting House: A facility where mined ore is sorted and separated based on its quality and mineral content before further processing.

Ore Washer: A person who washes and separates valuable minerals from dirt and debris.

Pan: A shallow metal dish used for panning gold or other minerals.

Pay Office: A building where miners would go to collect their wages or receive payment for their work.

Picker: A young worker who sorted coal or other materials based on quality or size.

Pickman: A child responsible for using a pickaxe to break coal loose from the coal face.

Pillar: A section of unmined ore or rock left in place to provide support and stability to the underground workings, often arranged in a grid-like pattern.

Pillar: A solid block of coal left in place to support the roof.

Pipefitter's Apprentice: A child learning the trade of a pipefitter, responsible for installing and repairing pipes in the mine.

Pit pony: Small horses or mules used to haul coal or materials in underground mines.

Pithead baths: Facilities near the mine entrance for miners to wash and change clothes.

Pocket: A small cavity or deposit of valuable minerals within a larger rock formation.

Powder Magazine: A secure building used to store explosive materials, such as black powder or nitroglycerin, needed for underground blasting operations.

Powder Monkey: Workers who assisted the shot firer by preparing explosive charges and handling detonators.

Powderman: A person who handles and stores explosive materials used in blasting.

Powerhouse: A building that houses the power generation equipment, such as steam engines or turbines, to provide electricity for the mine and its operations.

Prop: A wooden or metal support used to reinforce the roof or walls.

Prospector: An individual who searches for mineral deposits, often in unexplored areas.

Puddler: A child who mixed clay and water to create a paste used for sealing mine walls.

Pump House: A structure or building containing pumps used to remove water from the mine, ensuring a dry working environment.

Pumpman: Skilled workers who operated and maintained the mine's water pumps, keeping the underground areas dry.

Quartz: A hard, crystalline mineral commonly associated with gold and other valuable ores.

Raise: A vertical or inclined excavation driven from one level to another within the mine, allowing for the movement of miners, equipment, and materials between different levels.

Raise Bore: A drilling technique used to excavate a vertical or inclined raise from one level to another, often utilizing a large-diameter drilling rig.

Raise Climber: A mechanical device used for vertical transportation in a raise, allowing miners to ascend or descend between different levels.

Raise: A vertical excavation that connects different levels within the mine.

Ramps: Inclined tunnels or roadways used for vehicular transport or the movement of equipment within the mine.

Rib: The vertical wall of coal or rock separating two tunnels or drifts.

Rock bolt: A long steel bolt used to reinforce the roof or walls.

Rockman: A miner who specializes in the extraction of ore or minerals from solid rock.

Roof fall: The collapse of rock or coal from the roof of a mine.

Roof: The overhead rock or strata above the coal seam.

Runner: A child worker responsible for running errands, delivering messages, or performing other small tasks.

Safety Inspector: A person responsible for inspecting mine conditions and enforcing safety regulations.

Safety lamp: A lamp with a protected flame used to detect the presence of methane gas.

Safety timber: Large timbers used to support the roof in areas of potential roof fall.

Scale: A mechanical apparatus equipped with a platform and counterweights to accurately measure the weight of extracted ore or materials

Scale House: A building or structure equipped with scales used to weigh incoming and outgoing materials, such as ore, coal, or supplies.

Scaler: A young worker who examined mine

walls and roofs to identify loose rocks or potential hazards.

Shaft: A vertical or inclined excavation used to access different levels or depths of the underground mine, often equipped with a hoisting system for transporting miners, materials, and ore.

Shaft House: A building located above the entrance of a mine shaft, used for housing hoisting equipment and providing access to the underground mine.

Shaft Sinker: A skilled worker responsible for sinking and maintaining vertical mine shafts.

Shaft: A vertical or inclined excavation used to access underground mines.

Shift Boss: The individual in charge of a specific shift of miners.

Shift Caller: An individual who announces the start and end of mining shifts.

Shot Firer: The individual responsible for setting and detonating explosive charges used in blasting operations to extract coal.

Shot Firer's Assistant: Workers who assisted the shot firer by preparing and setting up explosive charges.

Shot Putter: Workers responsible for placing and tamping explosive charges in the drilled holes for blasting operations.

Shovel: A manual tool used to load coal into mine cars or conveyors.

Signal House: A building where signaling equipment, such as bells, whistles, or sirens, is located to communicate with workers in the mine.

Sinker: A young worker involved in the sinking of mine shafts or the digging of mine tunnels.

Slag Heap: An area or mound near the smelter where waste material, called slag, is dumped and accumulated after the smelting process.

Slate Picker (in Breaker): A child employed

to separate slate or other impurities from the mined coal in the Coal Breaker building.

Slate Picker: Workers who manually removed slate and other non-coal materials from the coal face before it was extracted.

Slate Runner: A child responsible for removing slate or waste materials from the mine.

Sluice box: A long, narrow channel used to wash placer deposits and separate heavy minerals.

Smelter: A building or furnace used to melt and refine the extracted ore, separating impurities and extracting metals through a process called smelting.

Stables: A structure or building topside where horses and mules used in mining operations are housed, fed, and cared for.

Stacker: A young worker who organized and stacked bags or piles of coal at the surface.

Stamp mill: A machine that crushes ore by pounding it with heavy iron stamps.

Stampede: A sudden rush or movement of miners in response to a new discovery or rumor of valuable deposits.

Stope: A working area within a mine where ore is extracted, typically formed by excavating a void or chamber in the mineral deposit.

Stope Filler: A laborer who fills empty mining areas with waste rock to support the mine structure.

Stope: A section or excavation within the mine where ore is extracted.

Sublevel: A horizontal tunnel or level situated below the main drift, typically used for extraction or exploration purposes.

Sublevel Stope: A specific stope located on a sublevel, often characterized by a series of interconnected working areas.

Sump: A low-lying area or cavity in the mine where water collects and is drained, helping to maintain a drier working environment.

Sump Pump: A pump used to remove water

from sumps or low-lying areas in the mine to maintain a dry working environment.

Supply Store: A building or shop where miners can purchase essential supplies, tools, clothing, and other items necessary for their work.

Surveyor: A specialist who measures and maps underground tunnels and mining areas.

Tailings Pond: A containment area where the waste material, called tailings, from the mining and milling process is stored to prevent environmental contamination.

Tailings: The waste material left over after the valuable minerals have been extracted.

Tamping: The process of packing explosives into drill holes.

Timber Framer: A skilled worker responsible for constructing and maintaining timber support structures.

Timber Inspector: Employees who inspected the mine's timber supports, ensuring their structural integrity and safety.

Timbering: The process of supporting the roof and walls of a mine with timber.

Timberman: Skilled workers responsible for the construction and maintenance of timber supports in underground mine shafts.

Timekeeper's Office: A building where the mine's timekeeper or timekeeping department is located, responsible for tracking and recording workers' hours.

Tip Boy: A child who collected and transported the coal and waste from the mine to the surface.

Tipping bucket: A device used to measure the quantity of water pumped out of a mine.

Tipple Worker: Employees stationed at the tipple (loading platform) who loaded coal onto rail cars for transportation to market.

Tipple: A structure where coal is sorted, graded, and loaded onto trains or trucks.

Tippler: Individuals who operated the tipple machinery, which tilted coal wagons to unload their contents into the sorting and processing area.

Tool Shed: A small building used for storing and organizing various mining tools, including picks, shovels, hammers, and other hand tools.

Track Layer: Workers responsible for laying and maintaining the tracks used by mine carts or wagons for transportation within the mine.

Trammer: A laborer who manually transports ore or waste rock from the mining face to the surface.

Trapper: A child employed to open and close trapdoors or gates in the mine to allow coal carts to pass through.

Tunnel: A horizontal passage within a mine used for access, ventilation, or transportation.

Vein: A narrow deposit of minerals that is typically oriented along fractures in rock.

Ventilation Engineer: An expert who designs and maintains the ventilation systems in the mine to ensure fresh air supply.

Ventilation: The circulation of fresh air in a mine to provide breathable conditions.

Warehouse: A building used for storing various mining supplies, equipment, spare parts, and other materials required for day-to-day operations.

Water Tower: A tall structure used to store and supply water for various mining operations, such as steam generation and dust suppression.

Weighman: Workers responsible for weighing and recording the amount of coal extracted from the mine before it was transported.

Winch: A device used to lift heavy loads in the mine, such as ore carts or machinery.

Winze: A vertical or inclined shaft that connects two levels within the mine, often used for ventilation or as an additional access route.

Workface: The active area within the mine where miners are currently extracting ore.

RESOURCES

A Coal Manual for Salesmen, Buyers and Users, Francis Rawle Wadleigh, (1921)

A Descriptive Treatise on Mining Machinery, George Guillaume André, (1881)

A descriptive treatise on mining machinery, tools, and other appliances used in mining, George Guillinane André, (1881)

A Glossary of the Mining and Mineral Industry, Albert Hill Fay, (1920)

A Guide to the Great Exhibition Containing a Description of Every Principal Object of Interest with a Plan... Examining the Contents of the Crystal Palace, (1864)

A History and Description of the Manufacture and Mining of Salt in New York State, Charles Jolly Werner, (1918)

A History of Coal, Coke, Coal Fields, Progress of Coal Mining, the Winning and Working of Collieries, Household, Steam, Gas, Coking and Other Coals, of the Great Northern Coal Field, Mine Surveying and Government Inspection, William Fordyce, (1860)

A History of the Coal Miners of the United States, from the Development of the Mines to the Close of the Anthracite Strike of 1902, Andrew Roy, (1908)

A History of the Lehigh Coal and Navigation Company, Lehigh Coal and Navigation Company, (1857)

A Journal of the Overland Route to California! and the Gold Mines, Lorenzo D. Aldrich, (1864)

A Manual of Mining, Magnus Colbjørn Ihlseng, (1894, 1900)

A Manual of Mining, Magnus Ihlseng, (1912)

A New Method for the Treatment of Mixed Copper, Silver and Gold Ores, James Douglas, (1880)

A Practical Manual of Minerals, Mines, and Mining, Henry Stafford Osborn, (1896)

A Practical Treatise on Coal Mining, George Guillaume André, (1883)

A Practical Treatise on Hydraulic Mining in California, Augustus Jesse Bowie (Jr.), (1888)

A practical treatise on the manufacture and distribution of coal-gas, Samuel Clegg, (1857)

A Practical Treatise on the Manufacture and Distribution of Coal-Gas, Samuel CLEGG (Civil Engineer, the Younger.), (1874)

A Revision of the Bituminous Coal Measures of Clearfield County, Henry Martyn Chance, (1887)

A Study of Coal Mine Haulage in Illinois, Harry Harkness Stoek, James Russell Fleming, Arthur Joseph Hoskins, (1922)

A Summary Description of the Geology of Pennsylvania: pt. 1. Carboniferous formation, J. Peter Lesley, (1896)

A Text-book of Coal-mining, Herbert William Hughes, (1893, 1900)

A Treatise on Coal Mining, International Correspondence Schools, (1902)

A Treatise on Earthy and Other Minerals and Mining, David Christopher Davies, (1887)

A Treatise on the Blasting and Quarrying of Stone for Building and Other Purposes, Sir John Fox Burgoyne, (1896)

A Trooper's Narrative of Service in the Anthracite Coal Strike, Stewart Culin, (1902, 1905)

American Coal Miner, (1920)

American mining & metallurgical manual, (1921)

American Mining Code, Embracing the United

States, State, and Territorial Mining Laws, and the General Land Office Regulations, Henry Norris Copp, (1905, 1906)

An Investigation of the Iron Ore Resources of the Northwest, William Harrison Whittier, (1918)

An Investigation of the Iron Ore Resources of the Northwest, University of Washington. Bureau of Industrial Research, William Franklin Allison, William Harrison Whittier, Jack Roderick Tolmie, Roy Odell Bach, (1918)

An Outline of the Geology of Floyd County, Kentucky, Willard Rouse Jillson, (1919)

Annals of Coal Mining and the Coal Trade, Robert Lindsay Galloway, (1900)

Anthracite or Hard Coal, (1921)

Blowpiping, Mineralogy, Assaying, Geology, Prospecting, Placer and Hydraulic Mining, (1905)

Boom Copper - The Story Of The First U.S. Mining Boom, Angus Murdoch, 2013)

Brief Description of the Anthracite Coal Fields of Pennsylvania, Charles Albert Ashburner, (1887)

California Journal of Mines and Geology, (1892, 1895, 1898)

Canadian Mining Journal, (1920, 1922)

Charter and By-laws of the New Jersey Slate-Mining and Manufacturing Company ... Together with a Geological Report, Testimonials, etc, New Jersey Slate-Mining and Manufacturing Company, (1858)

Charter, Coal Fields, Family Plans, for Supplying Each Shareholder with the Best Coal in Pennsylvania, Summit Branch Railroad Company, (1869)

Coal Report of Illinois, (1893)

Coal, John Adams Bownocker, (1909)

Coal Age, (1913-1923)

Coal and Coke, Frederick Henry Wagner, (1909, 1917)

Coal and the Coal Mines, Homer Greene, (1891)

Coal Deposits of Iowa, Charles Rollin Keyes, (1895)

Coal Fields of Grand Mesa and the West Elk Mountains, Colorado, Willis Thomas Lee, (1913)

Coal Handling Machinery, C.W. Hunt Company, (1894)

Coal Men of America, Arthur M. Hull, Sydney A. Hale, (1919)

Coal Mine Management, (1923)

Coal Miners' Pocketbook, Thomas J. Foster, (1917)

Coal Mines, (1910, B. H. Rose, (1911)

Coal Mining Catalogs, (1918)

Coal Mining in Arkansas, Alvin Arthur Steel, (1911)

United States. Congress. House. Committee on Mines and Mining, (1915)

Copper Curb and Mining Outlook, (1915, 1917)

Copper Mining in Lake Superior. ..., Thomas Egleston, (1882)

Cost of Production: Iron, Steel, Coal, etc, United States. Bureau of Labor, (1893)

Dana's Manual of Mineralogy for the Student of Elementary Mineralogy, the Mining Engineer, the Geologist, the Prospector, the Collector, Etc, James Dwight Dana, (1913)

Description of Valuable Coal, Iron Ore, Lumber, and Farm Lands, in Somerset County, Pennsylvania, (1873)

Dictionary of Manufactures, Mining Machinery, and the Industrial Arts, George Dodd, (1880, 1880)

Dredging for Gold in California, D'Arcy Weatherbe, (1907)

Engineering and Mining Journal, (1878-1923)

Economic Geology of the Beaver Quadrangle, Pennsylvania (southern Beaver and Northwestern Allegheny Counties), Lester Hood Woolsey, (1906)

Economic Geology of the Georgetown Quadrangle (together with the Empire District) Colorado, Josiah Edward Spurr, George H. Garrey, Sydney Hobart Ball, (1909)

Economic Geology of the Mercur Mining District, Utah, Josiah Edward Spurr, (1896)

Economic Mining, Charles George Warnford Lock, (1895)

Elements of Mining, George Joseph Young, (1917)

Elements of Mining Geology and Metallurgy (illustrated), George Washington Miller, (1907)

Engineering Features of Missabe Range Mining, Earl Emmet Hunner, (1908)

Engineering Mechanics Devoted to Mechanical Civil, Mining and Electrical Engineering,
(1893)

Explosives for Quarrying, E.I. du Pont de Ne-
mours & Company, (1921)

Exposition Concerning the Mineral Coal of
Michigan. March 1854, Richard Ray Lan-
sing, (1867)

Family scenes in a mining district, by a resident, Family scenes, (1863)

Financial and Mining Record, (1893)

First Report of Progress in the Anthracite Coal
Region, Charles Albert Ashburner, (1886)

Fremont County at the Grand National, Mining
and Industrial Exposition, at Denver, Colorado, (1882, (1885)

Gas Poisoning in Mining and Other Industries,
John Glaister, David Dale Logan, (1915)

Geological Survey Of Michigan. Upper Peninsula 1869-1873 Accompanies By An Atlas Of Maps. Vol. I., (1879)

Geology and Coal Fields of the Lower Matanuska Valley, Alaska, George Curtis Martin, Frank James Katz, (1913)

Geology and Mineral Resources of the Western Coalfield, Joseph Edmund Carne, (1909)

Geology Applied to Mining, Josiah Edward Spurr, (1908)

Geology of the Aspen Mining District, Colorado, with Atlas, Josiah Edward Spurr, (1900)

Geology of the Castle Mountain Mining District, Montana, Walter Harvey Weed,Louis Valentine Pirsson, (1898)

Geology of the Lewistown Coal Field, Montana, William R. Calvert, (1910)

Geology of the Tonopah Mining District, Nevada, Josiah Edward Spurr, (1906)

God's Gold, John T. Flynn, 2007)

Gold and Tin Dredging Practice, Harold Langford Lewis, (1906)

Gold Dredging in California, J. E. Doolittle, (1906, 1911)

Gold Milling, Charles George Warnford Lock, (1901)

Gold Quartz Veins of the Alleghany District, California, Henry Gardiner Ferguson, Roger W. Gannett, (1984)

Great American Industries: Coal, Petroleum, Iron, Marble, Slate, Gold, And Silver, William Francis Rocheleau, (1904)

Guide to the Yukon Gold Fields, Veazie Wilson, (1896)

Hand Firing Soft Coal Under Power-plant Boilers, Henry Kreisinger, (1916)

Hand-book of Mining Law, Henry Norris Copp, (1882)

Harrison Improved Mining Machine ..., George D. Whitcomb, (1885)

Coal Mining in Pennsylvania, James Moore Swank, (1882)

Iron Mines and Mining in New Jersey, William Shirley Bayley, (1910)

Iron Mining in Minnesota, Charles Edwin Van Barneveld, (1913)

Iron Ores of Minnesota, Newton Horace Winchell, Horace Vaughn Winchell, (1850)

Jeffrey Material Handling and Mining Machinery: General Catalog No. 85, Jeffrey Manufacturing Company, Columbus, Ohio, (1924)

Judging Coal Values, Gerald Blenkiron Gould, (1922)

King Coal, Upton Sinclair, (1918)

Labor Relations in the Fairmont, West Virginia, Bituminous Coal Field, Boris Emmet, (1966)

Land Laws of Mining Districts, Charles Howard Shinn, (1887)

List of Coal Mines in West Virginia, West

Virginia Geological and Economic Survey, (1921)

Main building and annexes. Department I. Mining and metallurgy. Department II. Manufactures. Department III. Education and science, (1880)

Managing Industrial Solid Wastes from Manufacturing, Mining, Oil and Gas Production and Utility Coal Combustion, DIANE Publishing Company, (1995)

Manual of Coal and Its Topography, J. Peter Lesley, (1869)

Manual of Hydraulic Mining, Theodore Francis Van Wagenen, (1884)

Materials for the Mining Industry, 2012)

Methods and Costs of Gravel and Placer Mining in Alaska, Chester Wells Purington, (1905, 1906)

Mine and Quarry, (1912)

Mine Haulage; Hoisting and Hoisting Appliances; Surface Arrangements at Bituminous Mines; Surface Arrangements at Anthracite Mines; Percussive and Rotary Boring; Compressed-air Coal-cutting Machinery, (1903)

Minerals and Mining Laws of Wyoming, Wyoming, (1912, 1913)

Mines Statement and Goldfields Report, (1895)

Mines, Miners and Mining Interests of the United States in 1882, William Ralston Balch, (1885)

Mining, (1899, (1903)

Mining Accidents and Their Prevention, Sir Frederick Augustus Abel, (1891)

Mining American, (1906-1915)

Mining and Engineering Record, (1901)

Mining and Engineering World, (1911-1917)

Mining and Metallurgy, (1918-1922)

Mining and Milling in the Reese River Region, Central and S.E. Nevada, A. Blatchly, (1875)

Colorado from First to Ninth Session, Inclusive, Colorado, (1879)

Mining Magazine, (1867, 1871)

Mining Petroleum by Underground Methods, George Samuel Rice, (1984)

Mining Practices, Engineering and Mining Journal, (1920)

Mining Reporter, (1908)

Mining Rights in the Western States and Territories, Robert Stewart Morrison, Emilio Dominguez De Soto, (1905)

Mining; Journal of the Northwest Mining Association, (1903)

Monthly Bulletin of the Canadian Institute of Mining and Metallurgy, Canadian Institute of Mining and Metallurgy, (1922)

Monthly Statement of Coal-mine Fatalities in the United States, (1918)

Northwest Mining Journal, (1909)

Notes on Gold Dredging with Reference to the

Introduction of the Industry Into New South Wales, John Blockley Jaquet, (1898)

Notices of Mining Machinery and Various Mechanical Appliances in Use Chiefly in the Pacific States and Territories, for Mining, Raising and Working Ores, William Phipps Blake, (1878)

Oil-field Development and Petroleum Mining, a Practical Guide to the Exploration of Petroleum Lands, and a Study of the Engineering Problems Connected with the Winning of Petroleum, Including Notes on Petroleum Legislation and Customs and a Discussion of the Origin of Petroleum, Arthur Beeby-Thompson, (1916)

Operating Regulations to Govern Coal-mining Methods and the Safety and Welfare of Miners on Leased Lands on the Public Domain Under the Act of February 25, (1920 (Public No. 146)., United States. Bureau of Mines, (1922)

Ore Deposits of the Silver Peak Quadrangle, Nevada, Josiah Edward Spurr, (1908)

Ore Deposits of Utah, Bert Sylvenus Butler, Gerald Francis Loughlin, Victor Conrad Heikes, (1921)

Ore Dressing: Breaking, crushing and comminuting.-pt.2. Separating, concentrating or washing.-pt.3. Accessory apparatus.-pt.4. Mill processes and management, Robert Hallowell Richards, (1911)

Ore Dressing: Mill processes and management, Robert Hallowell Richards, (1911)

Pacific Mining News of the Engineering & Mining Journal-press, George Joseph Young, (1929)

Pacific Mining News. Supplement to Engineering and Mining Journal-Press, (1929)

Papers and Reports Relating to Minerals and Mining, (1902)

Pit & Quarry, (1919-1922)

Placer Mining ; Surface Arrangements at Ore Mines ; Preliminary Operations ; Ore Mining ; Supporting Excavations ; Assaying, International Correspondence Schools, (1910)

Pomeroy's Mining Manual for Prospectors, Miners and Schools, Henry R. Pomeroy, (1885)

Poor's Manual of Industrials; Manufacturing, Mining and Miscellaneous Companies, (1914, 1917, 1919)

Potash Lands and Potash Mining, United States. Congress. House. Committee on the Public Lands, (1919)

Practical Coal Mining, George L. Kerr, (1907)

Practical Coal-mining, William Savage Boulton, (1910)

Practical Gold-mining, Charles George Warnford Lock, (1889)

Practical Mineralogy, Assaying and Mining, Frederick Overman, (1867)

Principles of Mining, Herbert Hoover, (1911)

Proceedings of the Coal Mining Institute of America, Coal Mining Institute of America, (1903)

Proceedings of the West Virginia Coal Mining Institute, West Virginia Coal Mining Institute, (1911)

Prospectus of the Golden Hydraulic Company, Golden Hydraulic Company, (1890)

Prospectus of the West Virginia Iron Mining and Manufacturing Co, West Virginia Iron Mining and Manufacturing Company, (1837)

Pumping and Hoisting Works for Gold and Silver Mines, Joseph Moore (M.E.), (1877)

Quarry Accidents in the United States, Albert Hill Fay, (1919, 1921)

Report on the Coal Mines of the Monongahela River Region from the West Virginia State Line to Pittsburgh, Including the Mines on the Lower Youghiogheny River, J. Sutton Wall, (1888)

Report on the Coals of Maryland, William Bullock Clark, George Curtis Martin, B. S. Randolph, John Joseph Rutledge, N. Allen Stockton, W. B. D. Penniman, (1907)

Report on the Colorado Coal Field of Texas, Noah Fields Drake, Robert Andrew Thompson, (1895)

Report on the Mining Methods and Appliances Used in the Anthracite Coal Fields, Henry Martyn Chance, (1886)

Report on the Property of the Alice Gold and Silver Mining Company, Walkerville, Montana, William Phipps Blake, (1885)

Report Upon the Gold Placers of a Part of Lumpkin County, Georgia, and the Practicability of Working Them by the Hydraulic Method, with Water from the Chestatee River, William Phipps Blake, (1870)

Reports of the Inspector of Coal Mines of the Anthracite Coal Regions of Pennsylvania, Pennsylvania. Inspector of Mines, (1896, 1903)

Reports of the Inspectors of Coal Mines of Pennsylvania, Pennsylvania. Inspectors of Mines, (1895, (1897, (1898)

Reports of the Inspectors of Coal Mines of the Anthracite Coal Regions of Pennsylvania for the Year ..., Pennsylvania. Inspectors of Mines, (1896)

Revised Report on the Bituminous Coal Beds of Pennsylvania in Territory Adjacent to the Pennsylvania Railroad East of Pittsburgh and Erie, John Kilgore Johnston, (1914)

Rhode Island Coal, George Hall Ashley, (1915)

Rock Boring, Rock Drilling, Explosives and Blasting, Coal-cutting Machinery, Timbering, Timber Trees, Trackwork, (1908)

Rock Island Employes' Magazine, (1954)

Rock Quarrying for Cement Manufacture, Oliver Bowles, (1919)

Room and Pillar Retreat Mining, Peter W. Kauffman, Steven A. Hawkins, Robert R. Thompson, 2017)

Safe Storage of Coal, Harry Harkness Stoek, (1921)

Safety in Stone Quarrying, Oliver Bowles, (1916)

Shortage of Coal, (1919)

Silver and Gold: A Story of Luck and Love in a Western Mining Camp, Dane Coolidge, (1920)

Simplification of Sizes and Terminology of High Voltage Bituminous Coal (handled Over Docks at American Head of the Great Lakes), United States. National Bureau of Standards, (1981)

Six Months in the Gold Mines, Edward Gould Buffum, (1864)

Some Facts about Sulphur and Sulphur Mining, American Sulphur Mining Company, (1878)

Sources and Transports of Coal in the Duluth-Superior Harbor, M. Sydor, Kirby Stortz, 2016)

Sources of Limestone, Gypsum, and Anhydrite for Dusting Coal Mines to Prevent Explosions, Oliver Bowles, (1974)

Standardized Card of Accounts for the Iron Mining Industry, American Iron Ore Association, (1921)

Statistics of Mines and Mining in the States and Territories West of the Rocky Mountains, Rossiter Worthington Raymond, (1877, 1879, 1881)

Steam Shovel Mining, Robert Marsh, (1921)

Stratigraphy of the Bituminous Coal Field of Pennsylvania, Ohio and West Virginia, Israel Charles White, (1893)

Summer Birds of the Anthracite Coal Regions of Pennsylvania, R. T. Young, (1899)

Surface Management of Federal Coal Resources (43 CFR 3041) and Coal Mining Operating Regulations (30 CFR 211)., United States. Bureau of Land Management, 2014)

Technological Change and Productivity in the

Bituminous Coal Industry, (1920-60, Edgar Weinberg, 2007)

Tests for Gold and Silver in Shales from Western Kansas, Waldemar Lindgren, (1904)

Tests of Coal and Briquets as Fuel for House-heating Boilers, Dwight T. Randall, (1910)

The Anthracite Coal Industry, Peter Roberts, (1903)

The Assayer's Guide; Or, Practical Directions to Assayers, Miners and Smelters, for the Tests and Assays, by Heat and by Wet Processes, of the Ores of All the Principal Metals, of Gold and Silver Coins and Alloys, and of Coal, &c, Oscar Montgomery Lieber, (1909)

The Atlantic Gold District and the North Laramie Mountains, Fremont, Converse, and Albany Counties, Wyoming, Arthur Coe Spencer, (1918)

The Black Diamond, (1899-1936)

The Book of the Golden Jubilee of Flint, Michigan 1855-1905. Published Under the Auspices of the Executive Committee of the Golden Jubilee and Old Homecoming Reunion, Flint. Executive committee of the Golden Jubilee and old homecoming reunion, (1907)

The Central Gold Region, William Gilpin, (1871)

The Coal and Coke Operator and Fuel Magazine, (1914)

The Coal and Iron Resources of Virginia, John Daniel Imboden, (1878)

The Coal Catalog, (1921)

The Coal Dealers' "Blue Book" , (1922)

The Coal Field Directory, (1922)

The Coal Fields Of Kittitas County, Edwin J. Saunders, (1916)

The Coal Fields of the United States, John Adams Bownocker, (1979)

The Coal Industry, (1920, 1921, 1937)

The Coal Miner's Handbook, International Correspondence Schools, (1914)

The Coal Mines, Andrew Roy, (1881)

The Coal Mines of Pennsylvania, Frederick Edward Saward, (1884)

The Coal Regions of Pennsylvania, Eli Bowen, (1862)

The Coal Trade, Frederick Edward Saward, (1875-1921)

The Coal Trade Bulletin, (1896-1917)

The Colliery Engineer, (1900-1914)

The Cost of Mining, James Ralph Finlay, (1911)

The Domestic Uses of Coal Gas, William T. Sugg, (1888)

The Economics of Mining, Walter Renton Ingalls, Herbert Hoover, R. Gilman Brown, (1909)

The Efficiency and Performance of a Wile Gas

Producer Using Coke and Anthracite Pea Coal, Frank Benjamin Rowley, (1908)

The Elements of Mining Engineering, International Correspondence Schools, (1903)

The Elements of Mining Engineering: Dynamos and motors, electric hoisting and haulage, electric pumping, signaling, and lighting, electric coal-cutting machinery, (1903)

The Explosibility of Coal Dust, George Samuel Rice, (1913)

The Geology of Coal and Coal-mining, Walcot Gibson, (1910)

The Geology of Minnesota, (1903)

The Gold Mines of the World (2d Ed., (1902), James Herbert Curle, (1904)

The Gold Placers of the Vicinity of Dahlonega, Georgia, William Phipps Blake, (1871)

The Golden State and Its Resources, John J. Powell, (1879)

The Golden West, (1921)

The Gold-quartz Veins of Nevada City and Grass Valley Districts, California, Waldemar Lindgren, (1899)

The Gold-silver Veins of Ophir, California, Waldemar Lindgren, (1897)

The Heroine of the Mining Camp, Harriet Earhart Monroe, (1896)

The History and Development of Gold Dredging in Montana, Hennen Jennings, (1918)

The Hydraulic Gold Miner's Manual, T. S. G. Kirkpatrick, (1899)

The Iron Ores of Lake Champlain, Adirondack Iron Ore Company, (1875)

The Iron Ores of Minnesota, Newton Horace Winchell, Horace Vaughn Winchell, (1850)

The Iron, Coal, Gold, Marble... in Alabama, Georgia, Kentucky, Mississippi, North and South Carolina, Tennessee and Virginia, Southern Railway (U.S.) Land and Industrial Department, (1902)

The Juneau Gold Belt, Alaska, Arthur Coe Spencer, Charles Will Wright, (1908)

The Mining Advance into the Inland Empire, William Joseph Trimble, (1916)

The Mining American, (1903, (1917)

The Mining and Quarry Industry of New York State, New York State Geological Survey, (1912, 1915, 1918)

The Mine, Quarry and Metallurgical Record of the United States, Canada and Mexico, Mine and Quarry News Bureau, (1900)

The Mining and Smelting Magazine, (1873)

The Mining Bulletin, (1896)

The Mining Congress Journal, (1920, (1956)

The Mining Districts of the Western United States, James Madison Hill, (1914)

The Mining Engineer, (1896)

The Mining Industry and Review, (1899)

The Mining Industry, Production of the Precious Metals from the Earliest Time Down to the Present, National Mining and Industrial Exposition Association, Denver, (1885)

The Mining Investor, (1895, 1915)

The Mining Journal, (1895, 1902, 1907)

The Mining Journal, Railway and Commercial Gazette, (1888, 1893, 1894, 1895)

The Mining Magazine, (1917)

The Mining Magazine and Journal of Geology, Mineralogy, Metallurgy, Chemistry and the Arts, (1868)

The Mining Magazine and Journal of Geology, Mineralogy, Metallurgy, Chemistry and the Arts in Their Applications to Mining and Working Useful Ores and Metals, Thomas McElrath, William Jewett Tenney, William Phipps Blake, (1868, 1871)

The Mining World, (1912)

The Mining World Index of Current Literature, (1914)

The Nenana Coal Field, Alaska, George Curtis Martin, (1920)

The Northwest Mining Review, (1895)

The Pennsylvania Anthracite Coal Field, Harry Harkness Stoek, (1904)

The Playbook of Metals: Including Personal Narratives of Visits to Coal, Lead, Copper, and Tin Mines; with a Large Number of Interesting Experiments Relating to Alchemy and the Chemistry of the Fifty Metallic Elements ... With Engravings, John Henry Pepper, (1872)

The Practical Handbook for the Working Miner and Prospector, and the Mining Investor, John A. Miller, (1900)

The Practical Miner's Guide, John Budge, (1852)

The Production of Coal ..., Geological Survey (U.S.), (1894)

The Quarry Materials of New York--, David Hale Newland, (1918)

The Rampart Gold Placer Region, Alaska, Louis Marcus Prindle, Frank Lee Hess, (1906)

The Roy Stone Hydraulic Mining and Dredging Company, Roy Stone Hydraulic Mining and Dredging Company, (1884)

The Salt Lake Mining Review, (1917)

The Smokeless Combustion of Coal in Boiler Furnaces, Dwight T. Randall, H. W. Weeks, (1909, 1914)

The Stamp Milling of Gold Ores, Thomas Arthur Rickard, (1909, 1911)

The Story of American Coals, William Jasper Nicolls, (1899)

The Story of Coal and Iron in Alabama, Ethel Armes, (1912)

The Story of Iron and Steel, Joseph Russell Smith, (1910)

The Technology of Marble Quarrying, Oliver Bowles, (1918)

The Treasures of the Earth; Or, Mines, Minerals, and Metals, with Anecdotes of Men who Have Been Connected with Mining, William Jones (F.S.A.), (1876)

The Treatise on Metal Mining, International Correspondence Schools, (1902)

The Underground Haulage of Coal by Wire Ropes, Wilhelm Hildenbrand, (1888)

The United States Mining Laws and Regulations Thereunder, and State and Territorial Mining Laws, to which are Appended Local Mining Rules and Regulations, United States. Census Office, (1889)

The Young Prospector, or, the Search for the Lost Gold Mine, Edwin James Houston, (1908)

Through the Yukon Gold Diggings, Josiah Edward Spurr, (1903)

To Encourage the Mining of Coal, Oil, Gas, Etc., on the Public Domain, United States. Congress. Senate. Committee on Public Lands, (1916)

Transactions and results of the National Association of Coal, Lime, and Iron-Stone Miners of Great Britain, held at Leeds, November 9, 10, 11, 12, 13, and 14, (1863. [With an introduction by J. Holmes.], (1873)

Transactions of the American Institute of Mining Engineers, American Institute of Mining Engineers, (1891, 1893, 1899)

Transactions of the American Institute of Mining, Metallurgical and Petroleum Engineers, American Institute of Mining, Metallurgical, and Petroleum Engineers, (1914, 1915)

United States Annual Mining Review and Stock Ledger: Containing Detailed Official Reports of the Principal Gold and Silver Mines for the Year 1879, 1883)

Utah Gold, Christine Wilkerson, (1997)

Watson's Words in the Hartley Coal Mine, Thomas Watson (Miner), (1862)

West Virginia Coal Fields, (1922)

IMAGE CREDITS

A BIT OF AN ODDBALL

Newry Maine

[Riley And Newry Maine], Maine State Archives, Oxford County Atlas Published 1880. Page 93, 1880

Tourmaline

[Annual Report of The Board Of Regents Of The Smithsonian Institution for the Year Ending June 30, 1900. Report Of The U. S. National Museum, Government Printing Office, Washington DC, 1900

Ore Car

[A Treatise On Metal Mining Prepared For Students Of The International Correspondence

Schools Scranton, PA. Volume Iv], 1899, By The Colliery Engineer Company.

Miners at Camp

[Ross Grant in miners' camp], Garland, John, pseud. [from old catalog], Published Philadelphia, The Penn publishing company, 1918.

Digging Together

Hard Rock Miners. United States Alaska, 1916. Photograph. ttps://www.loc.gov/item/99614749/.

A FLIP OF A COIN

Comstock Mine

Story Of The Mine As Illustrated By The Great Comstock Lode Of Nevada By Charles Howard Shinn, New York D. Appleton And Company, 1897

Corliss engine at Centennial Exhibition

[Our centennial--President Grant and Dom Pedro starting the Corliss engine], Illus. by Theodore R. Davis in: Harper's weekly, 1876 May 27, p. 421. Library of Congress, Prints and Photographs Division.

Machines on Line Shaft

A view of the Pratt & Whitney display at the Vienna 1873 World Exhibition (Weltausstellung 1873 Wien) Created: 1876 "STEINHAUS f N.Y. [New York]" and "American Photo Lithographic Co. N.Y. [illegible]"A report published by the U.S. Government Printing Office, 1876.

John William Mackay

The Engineering And Mining Journal, Volume LXXIV July To December 1902, The Engineering And Mining Journal Incorporated 261 Broadway, New York

Improved Corliss Engine

[Improved Corliss Engine], Machinery for Metalliferous Mines, Second Edition (Rewritten and Enlarged), By E. Henry Davies, F.G.S. Mining Engineer, Van Nostrand Company, New York 1902

Morgan Silver Dollar

[Morgan Silver Dollar Coin], United States Mint, 1878-1921. Widely circulated.

A MAN WORTH HIS SALT
Warsaw Salt Works

[A History And Description Of The Manufacture And Mining Of Salt In New York State], By Charles J. Werner, Enlarged Edition, Illustrated, Published by The Author, Huntington Long Island, N. Y. 1917

Loading Salt

[BULLETIN OF THE New York State Museum VOL. 3 No. 11] University of the State of New York, April 1893

A STRIKING IMPRESSION
Cleveland Cliffs Mine

[Cliffs Mine A & B Shafts - Ishpeming, Marquette County, MI], Michigan Iron Mines, Used with permission, http://www.miningartifacts.org/Michigan-Iron-Mines.html

Ernest Hemingway

[Ernest Hemingway seated at typewriter]. Photograph. Arnold, Lloyd R, photographer. Retrieved from the Library of Congress, <www.loc.gov/item/2002736785/

ALL I WANTED WAS TO SEE THE SUNRISE

Trap Door

[Trapper Boy, "Son." Opens and closes a door that controls ventilation], Hine, Lewis Wickes, 1874-1940, photographer, Published 1908, Collection National Child Labor Committee collection, Repository: Library of Congress Prints and Photographs Division Washington, D.C. 20540 USA, Library of Congress Control Number 2018673769

Breaker Boys

[Boys in the Breakers], Anthracite Coal Communities, by Peter Roberts, 1904, pp.174-181

Coal Breaker

Author sketch

CONCRETE CITY

Concrete City Unit

Journal of the Engineers' Society of Pennsylvania; Papers, Discussions, Abstracts, Proceedings: Volume 6, Engineers' Society of Pennsylvania, Jan 1914 ·

Truesdale Colliery

[The Truesdale Colliery], The Colliery Engineer Vol XXXV – No 2, September 1914, Published by International Textbook Co., Scranton, PA

Concrete City – Recent

[An abandoned building in Concrete City, near Nanticoke, Pennsylvania, Highsmith, Carol M., 1946-, photographer, Library of Congress Prints and Photographs Division Washington, D.C. 20540 USA, Retrieved from the Library of Congress, <www.loc.gov/item/2019689900/

FOR PEAT'S SAKE
Digging Peat

[The Commercial Museum Handbooks to the Exhibits No. 3 The Peat Exhibit With The Uses Of Peat And Its Many Products] By Wm. L. Fisher, M. S. Assistant Curator of the Philadelphia Commercial Museums, Published By The Philadelphia Museums, 1920

Peat Digging Machine

[The Commercial Museum Handbooks to the

Exhibits No. 3 The Peat Exhibit With The Uses Of Peat And Its Many Products] By Wm. L. Fisher , M. S. Assistant Curator of the Philadelphia Commercial Museums, Published By The Philadelphia Museums, 1920

JIM AND HIS RESCUE ANGEL

Silver Bow County

"The Land of Opportunity" – 1919, By the Department of Agriculture and Publicity, Chas. D. Greenfield, Commissioner, Independent Publishing Company, Helena MT

Shaft and Timbering

A Treatise On Metal Mining Prepared For Students Of The International Correspondence Schools Scranton, PA. Volume IV, 1899, By The Colliery Engineer Company .

Miner Awaiting Rescue

[Timbering Of Metal Mines], By E. A. Holbrook, Richard V. Ageton And Harry E. Tufft, Department Of The Interior, Government Printing Office, 1923

Mine Timbering

[Square set timbering], Timbering Of Metal Mines, By E. A. Holbrook , Richard V. Ageton And Harry E. Tufft, Department Of The Interior, Government Printing Office, 1923

PEARL THE MINE MULE
Life at the Mule Farm

Farmers ' Bulletin No. 1341

U. S. Department Of Agriculture, Washington, D. C.

Issued August 1923, U.S. Government Printing Office

Pearl

Farmers ' Bulletin No. 1341

U. S. Department Of Agriculture, Washington, D. C.

Issued August 1923, U.S. Government Printing Office

Mules for Sale

Library of Congress, Prints & Photographs

Division, FSA/OWI Collection, [reproduction number, e.g., LC-USF34-9058-C]

Stock Car

[The Car - Builder's Dictionary, 3rd Edition, 1895, Compiled For The Master Car - Builders ' Association By Professor John C. Wai, M. C. E, The Railroad Gazette, 32 Park Place

Mine Cage

911Metallurgist.com, used with permission

Harness

The Engineering and Mining Journal, June 17, 1911, pg 1193

Preparing Pearl for Shaft

[Preparing a mule for the descent down a mine shaft]: mule on shaft elevator before descent, no. 8, Published c1908. Library of Congress Control Number **2006675529**

Mule Drift

[Mules in underground stable], Published c1906. Photo by H.J. Harris., Library of Congress, Library of Congress, Control Number 2016647682

Pearl Working Underground

{Man and beast toiling in perpetual night-- hauling coal to the shaft], M. & C. bituminous mines, Decatur, Ill., International View Co., Created / Published Decatur, Illinois, U.S.A., c1904.

Pearl Back Above Ground

[Miner and mule at American Radiator Mine, Mount Pleasant, Westmoreland County, Pennsylvania], Mydans, Carl, photographer, United States. Resettlement Administration. Published 1936 Feb,, Farm Security Administration - Office of War Information Photograph Collection (Library of Congress) Control Number 2017714734

THE POTS AND PANS REBELLION

Mother Jones

[Mother Jones], Bain News Service, publisher, Published Jan. 20, 1915

Mine Scale

[Diamond's Year Book and Directory, 1912], by The Black Diamond Co, Chicago IL.

Local Newspaper Coverage

Elmira Gazette of October 7, 1899

THE BUSINESS CAR

Drift Mine Section

Mineral Deposits of The Santa Rita and Patagonia Mountains Arizona, By Frank C. Schrader, Department Of The Interior United States Geological Survey, Bulletin No 582, 1915

Business Car

Bulletin of The American Museum of Safety January 1916 Published Monthly by The American Museum of Safety 14-18 West 24th Street New York

Business Car Design

Proceedings Of The Lake Superior Mining Institute Sixteenth Annual Meeting Menominee Range, Michigan June 22, 23 , 24 , 1911, Presses Of Iron Ore, Ishpeming , Mich

Fan House

[Properties Of Gases, Mine Gases, Mine Ventilation, Fuels], Reference Library, 92-139,

The International Correspondence Schools, Scranton International Textbook Company, 1907

ABOUT THE AUTHOR

I owe my existence to the underground mining industry. My grandfather worked and died in the coal mines in central Pennsylvania.

Our family's life changed dramatically in 1913 when he was killed in a mining accident in Arnot, Pennsylvania. His sudden death left my grandmother a widow at age thirty-seven with twelve children who would grow up without a father.

As I grew into manhood, I heard many stories about my grandfather, who was a proud and industrious man, unafraid of danger or hard work. The way he lived and worked was an inspiration to his children and grandchildren. We all entered adulthood equipped with the same grit and determination which enabled our grandparents to survive and give us the gift of life.

I am proud to have that DNA.

In my long career, I have had the pleasure of working for one of the world's largest manufacturers of underground and hard rock mining machinery. This stage of my life provided me with the opportunity to become involved in underground mining "up close and personal" and to meet, learn and listen to the stories of miners from all over America. During this time, I received additional intensive training through the Penn State College of Mining and Mineral Engineering. This gave me a deeper understanding of our planet as I learned about its fascinating geological processes, its deep-time history, and the intricate interplay of the elemental materials which resulted in the world we know.

The American mining industry has undergone significant technological advancements since the nineteen century. The adoption of advanced machinery, automation, computerized systems and safety measures have dramatically improved efficiency, productivity, and worker safety. I feel blessed to have been involved in a small way in this transition.

Harvesting our earth's natural resources continues to play a crucial role in our economy, providing the essential raw materials necessary for a multitude of industries, including manufacturing, construction, energy, and technology. This massive effort continues to contribute to our nation's economic growth, job creation and our infrastructure development.

In this volume, I have sought to portray some of the people who were involved in mining in the late nineteenth and early twentieth century. All of these stories were inspired by documented accounts of actual individuals, locations and events.

Is all of it true? Who knows? Writing about what happened between the 1850's to 1950's requires the writer to take some literary license. Since I wasn't there to see these people and events in person, I have relied on accounts recorded by others. So I have taken what was documented and added some additional details that I hope will provide you with "the rest of the story", as the late Paul Harvey would put it.

When I was a kid, we did not have computers, digital devices and social media. Instead, I learned from the stories told by my elders. These tales went far beyond the two-dimensional narratives which appeared in newspapers, magazines, and journals of the day.

I was blessed to be part of this storytelling circle at home and later, in my working life, giving me a glimpse of a world which few will ever see.

Nancy, my bride of almost four decades, and our beloved fifteen-year-old cat, Lulu, continue to be my constant joy, support and inspiration.

My life-long respect and attachment to those who labor to extract the natural resources of our planet has inspired me to create this collection of stories to share with you.

I invite you to sit back and enjoy my book and come along with me on a journey back to the bygone days of the mining industry.

And if you'd like to read or listen to more of my other stories, visit my website at www.Jim-Kissane.com

YOU MAY ALSO ENJOY

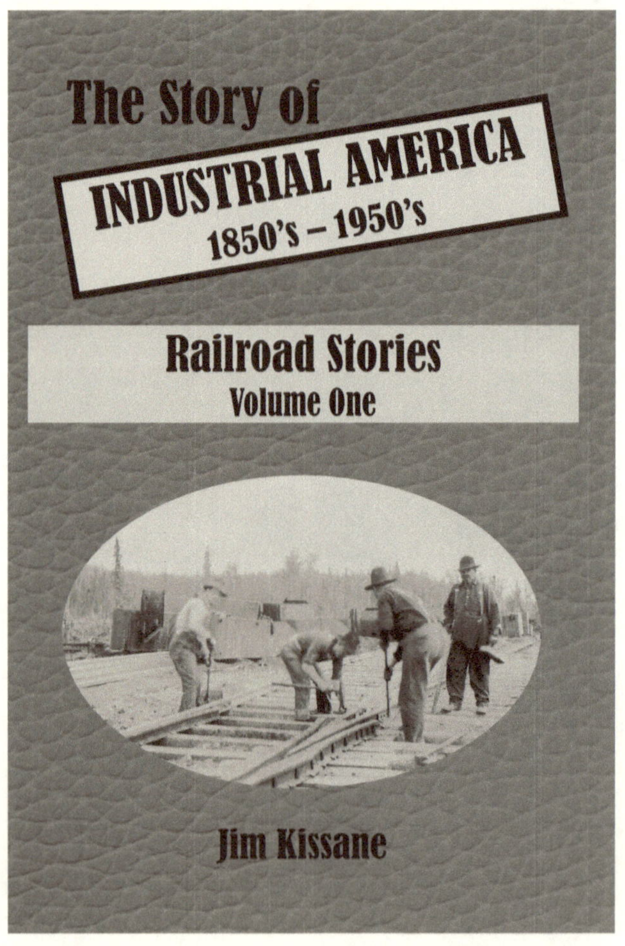